CHURCH LIFE

Paul E Brown

Grace
Publications

GRACE PUBLICATIONS TRUST
7 Arlington Way
London EC1R 1XA
England

e-mail: editors@gracepublications.co.uk
www.gracepublications.co.uk

© Grace Publications Trust

First published 2019
ISBN: 978-1-912154-17-3

Cover design by Stephen Talas

Printed and bound in the UK by Ashford Colour Press

*The author and editors are very grateful to Mrs Ruth Firth for
her helpful suggestions to make the book more suitable for an
international readership.*

Contents

Introduction

If 'Church Life' sounds unfamiliar, think of the phrase 'family life'. We are all individuals, with our own feelings and abilities; we have our own personal lives. The great majority of us, however, have also experienced family life. We grew up in the shared life of the family, and later most people also enter into a new family relationship. Similarly, the Christian life is lived by individuals, but it is also intended to be a shared life. It is a life lived together with our brothers and sisters in Christ; it is church life.

In the book of Acts we find that, on the day of Pentecost, those who came to believe in Jesus Christ as Saviour formed the church in Jerusalem. As the gospel spread, wherever groups of people believed they formed the church in the place where they lived. Nearly all the letters in the New Testament were written to churches in different cities. Even those that were written to individuals were still concerned with churches. The last book in the Bible, Revelation, was written to the seven churches of Asia. A large part of the New Testament is really about church life, which is the subject of this book.

In those early days there was only one church in each town to which the gospel had been brought. Each church was a local church; that is, it was the church of Jesus Christ in that place, that locality. There was no other church, nor could there be. This, of course, is not the case in these days. There are all sorts of different churches; in many countries towns have numbers of churches in them.

These churches generally have differences of beliefs and practices. Such differences are very important when they concern the inspiration of the Bible and the gospel message itself. This book is based on a belief in the divine inspiration of the Bible and its authority for every aspect of Christian doctrine and practice. Quite often, however, there is general agreement about the heart of the gospel message; differences are more about matters like church government or styles of worship. This book does not attempt to say anything about how these lesser differences may be dealt with; that is not its purpose. However, it does have in mind churches of a certain type and so this must be acknowledged here in the Introduction.

The churches in view are, firstly, independent churches. This does not mean that they have nothing to do with any other churches. Rather, each church recognises that it is governed by, and answerable to, Jesus Christ himself. The Bible is the Word of God and the church looks to it for the mind of Christ, and to the Holy Spirit for insight into Christ's will and grace to do what he says. The pattern for this is seen clearly in the first three chapters of the book of Revelation. Of course, a church can learn from other churches and from individual Christians, but only to learn the will of Jesus Christ as it is seen in his Word. Each church is accountable directly to him as its head and Lord.

Secondly, the book is also written with the understanding that baptism is for believers and not infants, whether or not these are the children of Christian parents. All the first male believers in Jesus who were baptised had already been circumcised as infants, receiving the sign of God's covenant with Israel. However, on believing in Jesus every one of them was commanded to be baptised in the name of Jesus (Acts 2:38) and this command continues for those born in the future and all who are afar off (Acts 2:39).

Thirdly, spiritual leadership in the church belongs to those who are described as elders, pastors or overseers. There are also others who serve in more practical ways and these are called deacons. A church should have some who serve by spiritual oversight and others who do so in more practical service.

These three aspects of church life are taken as basic, though more will be said about them later on. It is in churches of this sort that the book seeks to explain the nature, privileges, demands and blessings of church life. Most of what is said here will actually be useful for all churches that take seriously what the Bible says, even though they might not agree with every detail of interpretation.

Do not think that this book has been written so that every church may alter the way it does things simply to follow what is said here. Rather it is written to explore and set out principles from the Bible which may need to be applied in different ways in different circumstances. If change needs to take place this should be done sensitively, often little by little as the whole church comes to agree. Wise pastoral care is always needed in all the different stages and developments in church life.

No one book, apart from the Bible itself, can be simply applied all over the world. Churches which develop and grow in very different cultures may well apply principles from the Bible in different ways. It is important to follow what the Bible says, but when the gospel first comes to an area it may not be possible for groups of Christians to function exactly as they would like or as they will in time. It is also becoming more and more important for churches to be able to bring in fully people from different cultures and backgrounds. The aim is for every believer to feel at home in the church.

Chapter 1
Setting the scene

The church and the churches

Jesus said, 'I will build my church' (Matthew 16:18). What did he mean by this? First of all consider the word 'church'. This word looks back to the Old Testament. The people of Israel belonged together as a congregation; that is a distinct body of people that together belonged to the LORD. Very often the phrase 'the congregation of Israel' was used when the nation gathered together on occasions of special religious importance (see, for example, Deuteronomy 31:30 and 2 Chronicles 6:3).

The New Testament word also means a 'congregation' or an 'assembly', a gathering of people who because they belong together also come together. In Matthew 16 Jesus was teaching that a new congregation was coming into existence. This would be a congregation clearly related to him, 'my congregation' or 'church'. Jesus had asked his disciples who they thought he was and Peter had replied, 'You are the Christ (or Messiah), the Son of the living God' (v.16). Jesus then said, 'On this rock I will build my church.' I believe we can say with confidence that the rock is not Peter himself, but rather his confession of Jesus as the Christ and the Son of God. The church is built as people come to recognise and acknowledge from the heart that this is who Jesus is.

Jesus also said, 'I will *build* my church.' While it is true that his disciples would be sent out to make disciples from all nations and that there is still a responsibility for Christians to make the gospel known, yet in the end it is Jesus who builds the church. It is through his gospel and by his Spirit that the church grows and spreads out across the world. Moreover the church is unlike any other institution that exists at present; it lasts for ever. It is eternal, and even the gates of Hades cannot prevail against it (Matthew 16:18).

The fact that Jesus used the word 'church' or congregation, which had been used of the people of Israel, reminds us that all the first Christians were Jewish. On the day of Pentecost Gentile converts to Judaism were also included. Then as the gospel spread, Gentiles received the gospel too and were fully included in the church (see especially Ephesians 2 and 3). The church reaches out to those from every nation, but Romans 11 strongly suggests that before the return of Jesus Christ there will be a widespread turning to Jesus Christ on the part of the Jewish nation. In the end the church will contain 'a great multitude that no one could number, from every nation, from all tribes and peoples and languages' (Revelation 7:9).

Jesus is both God and man, and so the church is also called the church of God. Actually, Father, Son and Holy Spirit are all involved in the building and continuance of the church. Those chosen by the Father are called through the gospel by the Spirit and brought to faith in Jesus Christ, the Son. Considered in this way, the church consists of all who are trusting in Jesus Christ throughout all the ages of time.

The church is often called the universal church, the one church built up during time and lasting for ever. However, at present the one church makes itself known in different villages, towns and cities where the gospel is preached and people come to trust in Jesus Christ. So we read, for example, of the seven churches of Asia (Revelation 1:4), and of particular churches in cities like Jerusalem, Corinth and Ephesus. When Paul wrote his two letters to the church in Corinth he addressed it like this: 'To the church of God that is in Corinth'. It is similar to saying, 'to the English community in Asuncion, Paraguay' or to any group of people from one country who form a smaller community in another city in another land.

When Paul wrote to the Thessalonians he used a similar expression, but the other way round, 'To the church of the Thessalonians in God the Father and the Lord Jesus Christ'. That is, to the community of Christians in Thessalonica whose real home and position was 'in God and Christ'. Living for the present in Thessalonica they actually belonged to the eternal, spiritual church of the Father and Son. It is important for us to understand this relationship between the whole church of God and the local church. Most of this book is about the local church, as the New Testament itself contains letters written to local churches spread across the Mediterranean world of that day. But such local churches need to recognise that they are all expressions of the one eternal church of Jesus Christ.

Two matters need to be made clear at this point. Unfortunately, the present situation is seriously complicated. This is not only because there are many different local groups of various sorts all claiming to be part of the universal church. In addition to that, many churches and church groupings have altered their beliefs over the years and follow trends in the culture of their countries rather than the Bible, the Word of God. Even in such churches, however, there are generally numbers who have a living faith in Jesus Christ, though their understanding of biblical truth may be limited.

Secondly, those churches which are faithful to the Bible and the historic truths of the gospel are still divided up into many different denominational groups. Discussing these differences is not the purpose of this book. However, it is surely good for gospel churches that are geographically close together to develop good relationships and pray for one another. Perhaps on occasion they might work together or meet together where this is appropriate. Members of the universal church of Jesus Christ must surely love one another and desire the good of all, even when there may be a measure of disagreement on some matters of doctrine or practice.

In New Testament times there was just one Christian church in a city, it was the local church. This meant that some of the churches were of considerable size. This was clearly the case in Jerusalem (Acts 4:4; 5:14; 6:7), Corinth (Acts 18:10) and Ephesus (Acts 19:18-20). Churches in these days are not local in the same sense. They generally have their own distinctive beliefs and practices and consequently draw people to them who appreciate their particular qualities, and sometimes these come from a distance. This is understandable, but it can lead to a narrow and inward-looking attitude. To avoid this, we need to make an effort to love all our fellow-believers even when we cannot always agree with them.

In Ephesians 4:1-6 Paul says, 'I therefore, a prisoner for the Lord, urge you to walk in a manner worthy of the calling to which you have been called, with all humility and gentleness, with patience, bearing with one another in love, eager to maintain the unity of the Spirit in the bond of peace. There is one body and one Spirit—just as you were called to the one hope that belongs to your call—one Lord, one faith, one baptism, one God and Father of all, who is over all and through all and in all.' It is right for all Christians, from all churches, to live in the light of these words.

Becoming a member of the church

How does a person come to belong to the church? Before Jesus was taken up into heaven to return to his Father he told his disciples to remain in Jerusalem until they had received the promise of the Father, the Holy Spirit (Acts 1:4). When this took place on the day of Pentecost Peter preached a sermon to the gathered crowds in Jerusalem (Acts 2:14ff.). There were people from all over the Mediterranean world present, as well as Jews from Judea and Galilee who had come to celebrate the occasion. Peter preached about Jesus, his death and resurrection, and this had a powerful effect on many who were listening. This is what the Bible says at that point: 'Now when they heard this they were cut to the heart, and said to Peter and the rest of the apostles, "Brothers, what shall we do?" And Peter said to them, "Repent and be baptised every one of you in the name of Jesus Christ for the forgiveness of your sins, and you will receive the gift of the Holy Spirit. For the promise is for you and for your children and for all who are far off, everyone whom the Lord our God calls to himself." And with many other words he bore witness and continued to exhort them, saying, "Save yourselves from this crooked generation." So those who received his word were baptised, and there were added that day about three thousand souls' (Acts 2:37-41).

'What shall we do?' That was the question. 'We have heard about Jesus, we have been cut to the heart because we rejected him and were at least in part responsible for his death, what must we do now?' Quite clearly they felt a sense of guilt and a need for forgiveness. How could that be obtained? Peter replied, 'Repent and be baptised every one of you in the name of Jesus Christ for the forgiveness of your sins.' There was an inward action needed, then an outward action. We start with the first.

Peter said, 'Repent'. The word means 'change your mind', or 'turn from one attitude to another'. It involves a turning from and a turning to. In repenting a person turns from sin and guilt, and turns to Jesus Christ. Both repentance and baptism are 'in the name of Jesus Christ'. Turning to Jesus Christ means trusting him, relying upon him as the only one who has made the forgiveness of sins possible. There is a real change of heart here. Conscious of guilt, a person turns in faith to Jesus Christ as the Saviour who gives us complete forgiveness. Such a turning is, of course, an inward thing. It is the heart turning from its own sinfulness to rest in faith upon Jesus. The person who truly does this becomes a real Christian and a member of the church of Jesus Christ.

Though repentance is the vital thing that brings a person to Jesus Christ, it is something inward. It will be seen in a new life and new behaviour, but it also needs to be confessed publicly. This will be a testimony both to believers and unbelievers of the inward experience that has taken place. It tells friends and family of the change that has happened. It is a public witness to them, and to the church, of faith in Jesus Christ. Repentance joins the believer to the eternal church of Christ. Baptism joins him or her to the local body of believers, the church as it is found in that place.

Peter called on every one to repent, but also to be baptised. The two belong together. Whether Jew or Gentile, whether male or female, whether circumcised or not, everyone was called to be baptised upon turning to Christ. This was to apply to children who in future days would hear the gospel, as well as to those far away who would hear of Jesus as the gospel spread across the world (Acts 2:39). The message was to be the same, 'Repent and be baptised.'

Baptists believe that this twofold call of the gospel is still the same today. What may or may not have happened to a child in infancy does not matter. Repentance, which necessarily includes faith in Jesus Christ, is essential to salvation. Baptism publicly shows that person is a believer and a member of the church of Christ and therefore, in particular, a member of the church in that place—the local church, the fellowship of believers.

Baptism, that is, immersion in water, is a picture of the spiritual experience of dying with Jesus Christ and rising with him to a new life as one of his followers. The old life has finished, a new life begins. It is lived by faith in Jesus and in the fellowship of others who belong to him. The passage from Acts tells us that three thousand were baptised and so they were added to the small company of believers that already existed in Jerusalem.

There was also a promise attached to this call to repentance and baptism: 'you will receive the gift of the Holy Spirit'. When does this take place? When a person believes in Jesus Christ, the Holy Spirit begins to dwell in his or her life. Acts 5:32 speaks of 'the Holy Spirit, whom God has given to those who obey him'. All those who obey the gospel call by repentance and faith in Jesus Christ, receive the Holy Spirit. From that time forward he lives in their hearts.

This does not mean that Christians will always have a sense of his presence and power in their lives; nor does it mean that there cannot be new experiences of his presence and help. Quite often when a person is baptised there will be a clear sense of the Spirit's nearness, and he may make the love of God very real, but this is not something which a Christian *must* have. As we shall see later, the indwelling of the Holy Spirit in all believers is one of the things that draws them and keeps them together.

The last verse in Acts 2 tells us this: 'And the Lord added to their number day by day those who were being saved' (v.47). In those early days the church grew very quickly (see also Acts 4:4; 5:14; 6:1,7). What is important here is to notice that those who were being saved were all added to the number of those who were already believers. They did not form separate groups or separate churches, or just remain individual Christians. *All* who believed were added to the existing church in Jerusalem. No-one just became a Christian and lived a life separated from the rest of those who believed in Jesus.

There have nearly always been Christians who do not belong to any local church. There are various reasons for this and some of these will be explained and considered later in the book. However, it needs to be understood that this is not what ought to happen. When people believe, they should belong to a church near where they live, and usually this will be where they heard the gospel. When Christians move to another place they should also join a church in the neighbourhood unless this is not possible. The Christian life is church life; life in a community of believers.

Basic biblical priorities of church life

We continue to look at what happened in Jerusalem on the day of Pentecost as recorded in Acts 2. Verse 42, following on from the baptism of three thousand people, says: 'And they devoted themselves to the apostles' teaching and fellowship, to the breaking of bread and the prayers.' The word 'devoted' shows the reality of the change that had taken place in the lives of those people. Everything was new, important and precious to them. They gave themselves wholeheartedly to the new life which was theirs now that they had trusted themselves to Jesus Christ. Four priorities in those early joyful days after they had experienced forgiveness are brought before us. These are also expanded on in the verses following.

First of all these new converts devoted themselves to the apostles' teaching. This does not mean that they held fast to what the apostles taught, because at that time they only knew a very little of their teaching. Rather, it means that they gathered eagerly to hear the apostles tell them more. The apostles were Jesus' witnesses (Acts 1:8). They were able to explain the life and teaching of Jesus and were also witnesses of his resurrection. So they would explain why he had to die, and how he had been raised, as well as many other lessons that they had learned from him.

All the teaching that Jesus had given them after his resurrection (Acts 1:3), the apostles would be able to pass on to those people who came to listen. The hearts of the listeners would be thrilled as they learned of Jesus' parables and miracles. They would be sobered and amazed that he had died for their forgiveness. They would be filled with joy at his resurrection and the promise of life eternal that that guaranteed. You can see by reading the letters to the churches later on in the New Testament just how much there was for them to learn. Today there is also much for us (all Christians) to learn!

An essential part of church life is receiving instruction in the apostolic teaching. This, of course, is found in the New Testament. Matthew, Mark, Luke and John have each given us an account of the life, ministry, death and resurrection of Jesus Christ. These four accounts complement each other, and each has its own style and emphasis. The letters of the New Testament show how the early churches received instruction both in teaching and practical life. How Christian faith works out in the individual life of the believer and the church community is clearly explained both by principle and example. Christian worship has always had a large emphasis on clear and practical teaching from the Bible.

Secondly, these young converts also devoted themselves to fellowship. Fellowship arises from a sense of a shared experience, a shared purpose and a shared destiny. These men and women had all been convicted of sin and had all received forgiveness through Jesus Christ. They had all been baptised into one community. These things separated them from everyone else in Jerusalem.

This does not mean they that ceased to have anything to do with other people, any more than belonging to one's own family means that you ignore the neighbours. Their new faith did, however, bring them into a relationship with people they may not even have met before, and put relationships with relatives and friends on a different footing. Something more about this will be said later.

Fellowship is much more than meeting together to listen to teaching. It is more than praying for one another. Verses 44-45 say: 'And all who believed were together and had all things in common. And they were selling their possessions and belongings and distributing the proceeds to all, as any had need.' This last phrase implies that some suffered as a result of their faith in Jesus. Perhaps some lost their employment; others may have felt that the way they earned money was incompatible with their new-found faith. And some, of course, would always have been very poor people. Whatever the precise reason, these new believers knew that they belonged together and so they helped one another according to need. This can be seen also in Acts 4:32 to 5:11. The important point to note is that they felt a unity with all other believers and lived this out in every way that was needed.

Thirdly, they devoted themselves to 'the breaking of bread'. This phrase can be understood in several ways. Firstly, it could be understood of the Lord's Supper, that is, it is a repetition of what Jesus instituted at the Passover with his disciples (Matthew 26:26-30; Mark 14:22-26; Luke 22:14-20; 1 Corinthians 10:16-17; 11:17-34; cf. John 13:13-30). Secondly, it could be simply be that they often ate together (see v.46). This would a sign of their oneness together. Thirdly, it could be that when they ate together, on at least certain occasions, they also remembered the Lord's death in the way he appointed. In other words, the Lord's Supper was part of a fellowship meal. The passage in 1 Corinthians 11 indicates that this was what happened at Corinth later on.

While the third option may be correct in describing how this took place, it is very likely that v.42 is simply saying that remembering the death of Jesus in the way he had appointed was one of the priorities of those early converts. They were taught to see that the death of Jesus was not a great tragedy and nothing more. Rather he had given his life as a ransom for many (Mark 10:45). As the good shepherd he had given his life for them, his sheep, but he had laid it down that he might take it again at his resurrection (John 10:11,17).

He had died for them; his death was the cost of their salvation, and remembering what he had done for them was of first importance. And it still is for the churches of Jesus Christ; we must never forget what we owe to him.

Fourthly, they devoted themselves to praying. We do not know exactly how they prayed, but it seems that when they met they would pray. We should note that the word is prayers; it is in the plural. It was not just that they prayed occasionally. There would be praying as well as teaching by the apostles. There would be praying when they remembered the Lord's death. Part of their fellowship was fellowship in prayer.

Verse 47 notes that they praised God. This may indicate that there was singing, most likely of Psalms, but it surely also shows that part of their praying included the praising of God.

Prayer is not just asking for things; Christians must always give thanks and praise to God for all his goodness.

It is interesting to note that singing is not mentioned in these four priorities. We live in days when singing often takes a major role in Christian services, sometimes there is more singing than anything else. We shall consider the place of singing later on, and its importance, but it does not feature here among the basic priorities. These are teaching, the Lord's Supper, fellowship and prayers; they all still need to have a central place in church life today.

Chapter 2
What, on earth, is the church for?

We have seen the beginning of the church in Jerusalem and the basic facts about its early life. There is no doubt that the church exists on earth and that there are many different expressions—or local churches—of the church in the world. But why has God chosen that those who have been forgiven their sins and who trust in Jesus Christ should belong to a worldwide body that shows itself in churches in many different places?

Perhaps it is helpful to start with some negatives. For those who trust in Jesus Christ belonging to a church is not something you can take or leave. Believing in Christ brings a person into the church and every believer is in the church and should therefore belong to a nearby church. Of course, in some situations a believer may be alone, simply because there are no other believers in the place where he or she lives. Sometimes, too, in countries where there is real hostility to the Christian faith, there can be no open church life. Even in such places, though, there are usually groups of people who meet in secret and who pray for each other.

We understand situations like that, but normally every believer ought to belong to a church. It is true that no church is perfect. It is also true that some churches are very far from being what the Bible says a church should be. In some cases Christians have found church life hurtful and distressing. In some countries Christians move from church to church and seldom fully commit themselves to any church because of their past experiences. In spite of that, and knowing that no church will ever be perfect in this world, God has his purpose for church life and it is right to seek fellowship and membership in a nearby church wherever possible.

Secondly, the church is not a Christian club or society, valuable though Christian Unions are in Universities and other institutions. It does not set its own rules or have its own agenda, or only accept those who it thinks are suitable. Nor is it, in normal circumstances, a secret society. It is an open society in the sense that its beliefs and rules, its priorities and its purposes are all set out in the Bible for anyone to read and understand.

Then again, the church is not designed just for certain kinds of Christian people. It is not a sort of spiritual hospital for weak Christians, though most churches will have Christians who need strengthening within its membership. Nor is it just for very able, outgoing people. It is intended for all who believe in Jesus Christ, whatever their strengths or abilities, their needs and weaknesses.

Fourthly, the church is not a man-made organisation, nor is it to be organised by what human beings may think is best. Unfortunately, some churches do look as if gifted and dominant people have made them according to their own ideas.

Finally, the church is not simply a social organisation. It is true that churches should provide material and social care for people in need, whoever they are and whatever their beliefs or un-beliefs. In serious circumstances churches should especially reach out with practical care for needy people. However, as time goes by, social concerns can sometimes become more important than the spiritual and this can lead to an almost complete change in the nature of the church. Those who serve in the church and its members need to watch out for this possibility.

The church has been given by God

We have already seen that the church is called the 'church of God' in the opening of both 1 and 2 Corinthians. In 1 Corinthians 10:32 this occurs again; in 11:22 Paul says: 'Do you despise the church of God?' emphasizing the nature and importance of the church. 1 Thessalonians 2:14 speaks of the churches of God, referring to local churches. The church is brought into being by God and the Father has placed it under his Son who becomes its head and Lord.

We must remember that God is a God of order. This is seen in all its magnificence in Genesis 1. The original creation was 'without form and void' but on the next six days God, in orderly sequence, made the world into a place of beauty and fruitfulness, displaying his glory and preparing it as a fit home for the people bearing his image. Sin has brought disorder into the natural world and into the lives of human beings. We know that human lives can sometimes be chaotic; most of us have some experience of that.

So the church has been brought into being by the God of order. God has given us guidance for the way the churches are to be structured and set up and arranged. Church life is not a matter of strict rules and regulations, but the Bible does give clear teaching which this book has been written to attempt to set out. The New Testament shows us churches that sadly became disorderly in various ways. Paul had to say to the Corinthians, with the conduct of worship particularly in mind, 'God is not a God of confusion, but of peace', 'all things should be done decently and in order' (1 Corinthians 14:33,40).

More than that; the Holy Spirit as the Spirit of Jesus not only dwells within each Christian but is also given to guide and empower the church as a fellowship of believers. In 1 Corinthians 3:16-17 Paul says to the church, 'Do you not know that you are God's temple and that God's Spirit dwells in you? If anyone destroys God's temple, God will destroy him. For God's temple is holy, and you are that temple.' The danger is that Christians often think of the indwelling of the Spirit simply in a personal, individual way. Paul here, however, is speaking of the Spirit dwelling in the church, guiding and instructing the whole body.

In Ephesians 4:1-6 Paul writes: 'I therefore, a prisoner of the Lord, urge you to walk in a manner worthy of the calling to which you have been called, with all humility and gentleness, with patience, bearing with one another in love, eager to maintain the unity of the Spirit in the bond of peace. There is one body and one Spirit—just as you were called to the one hope that belongs to your call—one Lord, one faith, one baptism, one God and Father of all, who is over all and through all and in all.'

The one Holy Spirit is given to the church in order to promote unity and harmony. As they grow together in faith and love all the members should come to have much the same mind, the same priorities, the same qualities and emotions because they are all indwelt and guided by the same Spirit. They all desire God's glory; they all desire the welfare and spiritual growth of each other. They all want love and godliness to flourish, they all want to work together; they all want to see conversions. The Holy Spirit of the God of order dwells in the church. The church should be different from all other organisations because it is God's creation; it is not a human club or just an idea that Christians have thought up. There is a serious challenge here to recognise the nature of the church and to live by the Spirit.

The church is the new humanity

The God who made the world also made the first human couple, Adam and Eve. If they had obeyed God they would have been the beginning of a humanity which lived to the glory of God and for the fulfilling of his purposes in the world. Sadly, this did not take place, they fell by disobedience and humanity has been sinful and alienated from God ever since.

But the coming of Jesus Christ signalled the beginning of a new humanity, one that would be made up of those redeemed by his sacrifice and born again by his Spirit. The most important passage on this theme comes in 1 Corinthians: 'For as by a man came death, by a man has come also the resurrection of the dead. For as in Adam all die, so also in Christ shall all be made alive.' 'Thus it is written, "The first man Adam became a living being"; the last Adam became a life-giving spirit. But it is not the spiritual that is first but the natural, and then the spiritual. The first man was from the earth, a man of dust; the second man is from heaven. As was the man of dust, so also are those who are of the dust, and as is the man from heaven, so also are those who are of heaven. Just as we have borne the image of the man of dust, we shall also bear the image of the man of heaven' (1 Corinthians 15:21-22 and 45-49).

This is a very important truth, which has very practical applications. It is quite clear that the old humanity, to which we all once belonged, is marked by many serious failings. Though we all came from one family at the beginning, history has been marked by jealousy, hatred, discrimination, violence and terrible wars in which millions of people have spent their energies and resources in killing one another. In spite of the United Nations, in spite of education and civilisation, all over the world there are tensions, uprisings, terrorism and war. There seems to be no answer to all these awful things, nor does one exist, except in the gospel of Jesus Christ.

Through Jesus Christ we are born again into the new humanity. There are three realities that all Christians need to take seriously. Firstly, there is a real unity and sense of belonging on the part of Christians. In many different parts of the world it is possible to find churches of Jesus Christ and to be welcomed and to know that you belong, even where there may be cultural differences. Many churches these days are multicultural; you will find people from many different backgrounds and ethnicities worshipping together. This is evidence that we belong to Christ's new humanity and it is a joy to experience this reality.

However, secondly, we have to say that while this sense of unity is real it is often far from perfect. The Christian world is divided up into a huge number of denominations and groupings and this, in itself, may seem to deny the claim that we form a new humanity. Of course, some of the differences between churches are not great and Christians often need to remember that we may never completely agree about matters that are not vital. Sadly, however, even within the same churches tensions can easily arise. It is true that we will never agree with every other Christian until Jesus Christ returns, but often there is too much criticism of others, suspicion and unkind and unworthy attitudes. Individual churches split and sometimes split again; brother falls out with brother and often no one seems willing to be humble enough to apologise and put things right. And we too often allow racial, national and cultural differences to affect our church life more than we ought.

So, thirdly, we need to understand that Christianity is the movement of God by which he is bringing peoples from every nation and ethnicity into his new humanity. While there is no easy road into complete harmony, at least we need to understand what God is doing and seek to bend our wills and our efforts to make the truth understood and show its reality. And, in spite of our human failures in the present, the new humanity will reach its perfection one day.

Before we take this theme further, there is something else we ought briefly to consider. We might have thought that when God called Abraham, or more particularly his grandson, Jacob (Israel), he was beginning a new humanity. After all, a great deal of the Bible is about God's dealings with the nation of Israel and in particular with the tribe of Judah, the Jews. However, the primary purpose of the calling of Israel was that this was the line from which would come Jesus, the Christ, the Saviour of the world.

But the history of Israel also shows us that God's new humanity can never be one which simply depends on natural birth. In spite of all God's mercies, the laws he gave them, the priesthood and way of forgiveness through sacrifice, again and again Israel departed from his ways. In the end it was the High Priest himself, together with the whole Sanhedrin, who condemned the Son of God to death (e.g. Mark 14:62-64). The new humanity can never be brought about by the old way of natural birth; as Jesus said, 'You must be born again' (John 3:7). Christians, too, need to remember this. So whatever our nationality or our status the way into the new humanity is through repentance and faith in Jesus Christ.

A new humanity needs a new place in which to live, and this is the promise of the Bible for the future: 'And I saw a new heaven and a new earth, for the first heaven and the first earth had passed away' (Revelation 21:1). So what is God doing now? He is preparing his people for their new home. Church life can sometimes be difficult at present. Christians saved out of the world have had their sins forgiven, but there is always much to learn and much that needs to be 'put right'.

God has to deal rather drastically with most of us because we cling on to the old life and the old ways. He does not allow his people just to go on much as they used to be before they were saved, and then suddenly transform them so that they are fit for heaven. He begins the work of changing our hearts and lives, our attitudes and actions, right now and we often find the process painful. A good chapter to read on this subject would be 2 Corinthians 4. It finishes like this: 'So we do not lose heart. Though our outer self is wasting away, our inner self is being renewed day by day. For this light momentary affliction is preparing for us an eternal weight of glory beyond all comparison, as we look not to the things that are seen but to the things that are unseen. For the things that are seen are transient, but the things that are unseen are eternal' (vv.16-18).

The local church is the place where we receive spiritual teaching, guidance and pastoral care

At this point we turn to consider why God has brought the church into being. It is in the church that people are prepared for the world to come. As we can see from the end of Acts 2, from the very beginning God has appointed in the church some who will teach those who are joined to it. The New Testament letters, most of which were written by Paul, are written preaching to churches. We can imagine the groups of Christians in Rome, Corinth, Ephesus and so on, gathered together when a letter arrived from the apostle. They would drink in Paul's words, though sometimes they might learn they have a need to repent and reform.

So it is that all through the history of the church there have been teachers and preachers of the Word who have explained and applied the Bible to the members. In a local church there can be systematic teaching, perhaps going through a book of the Bible or exploring a biblical theme. In this way members are encouraged, challenged, humbled, built up, and strengthened. In the church people do not pick and choose what they are going to hear; they do not simply listen to well-known or favourite preachers via the modern media. It is their pastor who brings the Word to them, someone who knows them, who meets with them, who is growing in his knowledge and understanding of the members. Church members often do not realise what a blessing it is to have ministry like this week by week.

However, while there is preaching in the church there is opportunity for much more. If there are things a member does not understand he or she can ask the pastor personally. As the pastor gets to know the people better he can direct his preaching more particularly to those areas where he knows there is ignorance, or where there are problems or questions. His preaching will become more and more suited to the congregation the better he gets to know them and to understand their situations and needs. He himself will grow in wisdom and understanding so the church will be blessed all round.

When there is illness or bereavement, when there are big decisions to make, when a member has fallen into sin, when someone has lost a job, when there are weddings or anniversaries, the pastor is there to share in the joys and sorrows, to give such guidance as he is able and especially to pray for his members. In numbers of churches there is more than one pastor or elder, there may also be a pastor's wife or a lady worker for women with particular needs. In the past, and perhaps still in some places, there used to be a family doctor who knew the family well and understood its medical needs. In the church there should be the spiritual equivalent. Jesus said to Peter: 'Feed my lambs' and 'Tend my sheep' (John 21:15-16). This is the work of the spiritual shepherd as a later chapter will explain.

The local church is the place where people learn to understand one another and learn from each other

Converts come from a great variety of backgrounds. Some will have been brought up in Christian homes; others may have come from the most ungodly of backgrounds. Some are young and others are much older. They will come from many different walks of life; they will have different experiences, different expectations and different temperaments. Some will be very outgoing; others will be quieter and may be shy. All this means it will not be easy settling into church life and working together with others.

To start with, however, everything is likely to seem wonderful. You have been saved. Jesus is real to you, your Saviour and your Lord. You share the same basic experience with all the other people in the church; you have so much in common. You love them and rejoice to worship together with them and talk of spiritual truths. But then things begin to alter. You notice things about them which are not so attractive, and very likely they notice things about you that are the same. Some of the weaknesses of the earlier life begin to show themselves. And suddenly relationships are not what they used to be.

However, in the church you have to learn how to fit together with one another. With the Bible in your hand and the Holy

Spirit in your heart you begin to learn to understand and to love the other members. At times you may find you have to accept them as they are. There may be things about their lives or their attitudes or their speech which distress you, but you need to be patient with them, for they are your brothers and sisters, they are fellow pilgrims on the road to heaven.

As you get to know each other better, you can begin to try wisely to help one another. You may not like it if others try to correct your faults, and the same may be true if you try to do the same to others, but gradually you learn that this is an important and needful process. This is part of what fellowship involves. This is one reason why God has put you into the church. You even begin to realise that if he had put you into a church where everyone more or less agreed with each other you would never really grow or develop.

Moreover, at the same time we begin to learn that God has made us different people. We are different physically, we are different temperamentally; we all have different abilities and disabilities. And so we have to make allowance for each other and also recognise that we are much better together than if every one of us was more or less the same. We have to learn to care for each other. We all have our weaknesses and we need to learn to encourage one another and pray for each other.

The fact that we can be very different means that we can work together to help one another. Those who are weak in one area of life are helped by those who are stronger. In this way we learn to grow together, strengthening and supporting each other. More experienced Christians can help those who are younger, while those who are elderly appreciate the care and thoughtfulness that those who are younger show to them.

There are believers who are severely disabled, yet in various ways their love for the Lord Jesus Christ shines out and they can be an inspiration to all who meet them. At the same time they usually have different needs to the majority which are not always recognised or met. Nor are churches always as understanding of such people as they should be; they do not always give them the help they need and this is harmful to the whole church. Church fellowship must include everyone and leaders, in particular, need to see that everyone in the church is cared for as far as possible and becomes integrated into the body.

The local church is the place where gifts and abilities can become clear and where there are opportunities to use them

Every Christian has gifts from the Lord. Some are multi-talented, others are much less gifted, but all are able to contribute in some way to the unity and work of the church. Gifts of speaking, leading and encouraging are all very obvious, and we thank God for those whose gifts are more clearly seen in the church, and which enable them to be a help to many. However, we should not only think of obvious abilities of that nature.

In Romans 12 Paul lists these among the gifts that are given according to God's grace towards us: serving, contributing with generosity and acts of mercy, which are done with cheerfulness. A little later on in the same chapter he speaks about brotherly affection, being patient in tribulation, contributing to the needs of the saints and showing hospitality. Amongst the fruits of the Spirit in Galatians 5 he includes patience, kindness, faithfulness, gentleness and self-control. Such gifts as these make a real difference to a church when they are seen and experienced and it is a great loss when they are not to be found.

We could look at other passages which mention other gifts and qualities which need to be developed and used, but these are sufficient to show us that the Holy Spirit gives a great variety of gifts to God's people. We should not concentrate too much on those gifts which are obvious and may give a few people some prominence in church life. We are to thank God for them, but look out also for the more spiritual qualities. There are some people who would be good speakers or leaders whether they were Christians or not. We are very grateful for them, but we also need to look for and seek to develop many other spiritual gifts and graces which make church life what it should be; something quite different from that which would be found in any other area of life.

The local church is the place where Christians serve each other and the world

As we shall see later, the local church is described in the Bible as a family. In family life the members help each other—or at least they ought to do so. Parents look after their children and bring them up as they would like them to develop. They want them to grow up as those who care for others, who use all the abilities and gifts that they have, who are not afraid of work. Children may sometimes quarrel, but the older should help and encourage the younger, they should care for and support one another. In later life they help and may care for their parents as these grow older.

Similarly, in the church, members should not only be concerned with themselves or their own families. They are in a wider family—one which contrasts with the smaller families which are more generally true of the Western world today. Within a church there are single people, older people, poor people, people who are unwell, individual Christians whose own families might be hostile to the fact that they are Christians at all. These are all brothers and sisters and to be viewed and helped as such.

All churches have a variety of activities. There are the usual services of the Lord's Day, but there are also likely to be meetings for children and young people, for older people, perhaps one for parents and toddlers, there may be special events. All these give opportunity for believers to get to know each other, to discover gifts and abilities and for love, understanding and fellowship to develop. Of course, Christians have to balance their lives—their work, family life, leisure and other aspects of life all have to be given their place. Different people, with different responsibilities, will have more or less time to give to the life of the church, but all should desire to contribute as much as is possible to its life and service for the Lord.

Christians, however, do not live in the church, but in the world and there they are to exercise an influence for their Lord. The ministry of the church and fellowship with Christians of different abilities and different forms of employment help to guide its members to grow as wise and useful members of society. While different from one another we can all learn from one another. We are not to try and copy each other, but we can learn principles and lifestyle choices from others which will help and guide us.

In the church we are also to learn from one another how to speak the gospel and to evangelise. Some have particular gifts of evangelism, others will have other gifts, but all need to learn the basic fundamentals of gospel witness to family, friends and neighbours. We should expect the church in its preached ministry, and by example and guidance, to impress on all its members that they are in the church and in the world as servants of Jesus Christ. Wherever we are, whoever we are with and whatever we are doing, we are still members of Christ's church and his servants. Our life is church life.

The local church is the place where discipline and sanctification take place

As we shall see, a church is to have structure, and it has those within who have authority to teach and guide its members from the Word of God. Belonging to Jesus Christ and being members of one of his churches means we have to accept the biblical standards of Christian behaviour and church responsibility.

You can get a flavour of what this means by considering what Paul says to the members of the church in Thessalonica: 'We ask you, brothers, to respect those who labour among you and are over you in the Lord and admonish you, and to esteem them very highly in love because of their work. Be at peace among yourselves. And we urge you, brothers, admonish the idle, encourage the faint-hearted, help the weak, be patient with them all. See that no one repays anyone evil for evil, but always seek to do good to one another and to everyone. Rejoice always, pray without ceasing, give thanks in all circumstances, for this is the will of God in Christ Jesus for you' (1 Thessalonians 5:12-18).

Because these directions are difficult to carry out, and often also because church members and their leaders sometimes get things wrong and act in ways which cannot be justified from God's Word, some believers prefer not to become church members, even if they attend the services of a church regularly. In some cases this may be understandable; but it is not what the Bible tells us. Christians who remove themselves from church life will almost certainly lose out in a number of ways even if they do not realise it.

In the early days of the church there were people who left the society of others and went into lonely places to be on their own and to devote themselves to prayer, fasting and the Word of God. Some of these were very devout, but they were seriously mistaken. We grow as Christians and learn holiness by interaction with our brothers and sisters. We do this by putting up with their immaturity and helping them with their weaknesses as well as by imitating their commitment to Christ and godliness of life. You cannot 'catch' holiness as you 'catch a cold', but you can encourage one another to greater devotion to Christ and wise, godly behaviour.

These last sections remind us that it is when the church flourishes and its members grow in holiness that it increases in its witness to the world around. There are many different organisations and clubs to be found, but the local church should be seen to be different from them all. The church should be reaching out in various ways to people beyond its borders, but its supreme impact should be seen in how the lives of its members are clearly changing and in the unity of love, goodness and purpose which it displays.

The local church prepares its members for heaven

Our life together in the church on earth is preparing us for the perfect life and fellowship of heaven. In Ephesians 5:25-27 we read: 'Husbands, love your wives, as Christ loved the church and gave himself up for her, so that he might sanctify her, having cleansed her by the washing of water with the word, so that he might present the church to himself in splendour, without spot or wrinkle or any such thing, that she might be holy and without blemish.'

Above all, it is the Lord Jesus, the head of the church, who, by his Holy Spirit, is at work in every local church. Through its leaders and the efforts and prayers of its members, the Holy Spirit is sanctifying each church and getting it ready for the day when every local church will be brought together into the one church of Jesus Christ in glory. That will be the day when all differences that we have now will have passed away for ever and the one Church will be the holy bride of its Lord. Churches must always keep this end in view. We are not simply trying to reform the world, nor are we competing with other churches; we are preparing ourselves, and being prepared, for the glory of our Lord and our eternal unity with him and all those who have been redeemed.

Chapter 3
Two pictures of the church

In the New Testament the church is described in a number of different ways using various comparisons. For example, it is compared to a flock, a temple, a bride, a city (e.g. John 10:16; 1 Corinthians 3:16-17; 2 Corinthians 11:2; Revelation 21:9-11). We do not need to look at all of these. There are, however, two very important ways in which the church is described: the church as the family of God and also as the body of Christ.

The family of God

In the first chapter of John's Gospel we read this of those who believe in Jesus Christ: 'But to all who did receive him, who believed in his name, he gave the right to become children of God, who were born, not of blood nor of the will of the flesh nor of the will of man, but of God' (vv.12-13). Christians, then, become the children of God; they are born into a spiritual family in which they become brothers and sisters.

There is an Old Testament background to this. The people of Israel were, of course, literally one large family. They were all descended from Israel, whose original name was Jacob. From his twelve sons came the twelve tribes, which all belonged together as a family under God their Lord. This was all in the plan of God. Genesis 35:10-11 says: 'And God said to him, "Your name is Jacob; no longer shall your name be called Jacob, but Israel shall be your name." So he called his name Israel. And God said to him, "I am God Almighty: be fruitful and multiply. A nation and a company of nations shall come from you, and kings shall come from your own body.'

It was important for the people of Israel to recognise their unity as a family. When God was giving instructions to the people in Deuteronomy he said this: 'You are the sons of the LORD your God ... For you are a people holy to the LORD your God, and the LORD has chosen you to be a people for his treasured possession, out of all the peoples who are on the face of the earth' (14:1-2). He also reminded them that they must treat one another as brothers and sisters: 'If among you, one of your brothers should become poor, in any of your towns within your land that the LORD your God is giving you, you shall not harden your heart or shut your hand against your poor brother, but you shall open your hand to him and lend him sufficient for his need, whatever it may be' (15:7-8).

The Israelites were a family by natural birth, but John's Gospel tells us that the church is a family by spiritual birth. The ties that bind Christians together are altogether deeper than those which bound Israel. All Christians have experienced a new birth; they are people with spiritual minds and a spiritual outlook. This should mean a deeper unity than we find in Old Testament days.

However, this is not the whole picture; something even greater than new birth into the family of God has taken place. Galatians 4:4-7 says: 'But when the fullness of time had come, God sent forth his Son, born of woman, born under the law, to redeem those who were under the law, so that we might receive adoption as sons. And because you are sons, God has sent the Spirit of his Son into our hearts, crying, "Abba!

Father!" So you are no longer a slave, but a son, and if a son, then an heir through God.'

Romans 8 adds to this: 'For you did not receive the spirit of slavery to fall back into fear, but you have received the Spirit of adoption as sons, by whom we cry, "Abba! Father!" The Spirit himself bears witness with our spirit that we are children of God, and if children, then heirs—heirs of God and fellow heirs with Christ, provided we suffer with him in order that we may also be glorified with him' (vv.15-17).

Adoption means that every Christian is an heir of God. Everyone is like an eldest son, all the riches and glory of heaven belong to every Christian by right. This is what the grace of God has done for us. In a human family in the past other children might envy the eldest son. This should not happen in the family of Jesus Christ. Whatever our position in this life, we are all heirs of glory, all equally accepted, adopted and wonderfully enriched by our heavenly Father.

So when we find that Christians are frequently addressed in the Epistles as 'brothers', all that we have been considering lies behind those words. This is how we should understand our relationship to all other Christians. If they belong to Christ, we are together with them in the same family. We need to know that Greek 'brothers' or 'brethren' very often means 'brothers and sisters'. When it refers to Christian believers in the New Testament this is nearly always the case.

A local church, then, is a Christian family both by spiritual birth and gracious adoption. We do not share the same blood, but we do share the same spiritual life and are indwelt by the same Holy Spirit. This presents a considerable challenge to members of any church. Hebrews 13:1 says: 'Let brotherly love continue.' And in his first letter Peter tells his readers: 'Finally, all of you, have unity of mind, sympathy, brotherly love, a tender heart, and a humble mind' (3:8).

It is true, of course, that family members may disagree with each other. Generally speaking, though, simply because they are family, they make up and put the past behind them. So sometimes there will be differences of opinion and outlook in the church family too. How the members then behave will show whether they understand their unity as brothers and sisters or not!

The body of Christ

The church is also described as the body of Christ (Ephesians 5:23; Colossians 1:18). This is true of the whole church, but it is also used to describe the local church as well (1 Corinthians 12:12,13,27). 'The body of Christ' is an astonishing description for a community of human beings. The church could scarcely be described in more exalted terms. That sinful people, even though forgiven, could be pictured as becoming so completely one with Jesus Christ that he could be called the head and his people the body, puts a remarkable honour on the universal church, and each local church. God the Father sees his chosen and forgiven people as united to his own beloved Son, as truly one as the head is with the body!

If Christians could only appreciate what a privilege this is it would transform their understanding of the church. To the world the church is just a group of people who happen to be religious. But if the church is the body of Christ in the world then his reputation depends on those who belong to it. This should impress upon them all the great importance of seeking, with the help of the Holy Spirit, to live up to that description. How sad it is that the body of Christ so often lives in a way that dishonours its head. If the members of the body bring shame and disgrace upon themselves, they also inevitably involve the head as well.

Christ the head of the body

It is the head that controls the body, for it is in the head that the mind is found. All the thinking and planning, all the attitudes and intentions are in the mind. For any human being, the body goes where its head desires it to go. It does what the head tells it to. Except in rare cases everything we do as humans is done with the consent and under the control of our heads. My fingers type these words because my mind tells me this is what I need to write at this point in the book. Sometimes the head tells a person that he or she needs to do something they would prefer not to do. Duty may sometimes be hard and the body may try to rebel against what it knows ought to be done. Except in times of illness the head is never against the body; and sometimes duty is unpleasant and difficult to perform. When there are things to do that are hard and difficult, the head also experiences and shares in the pain and tiredness that the body may feel.

It is just like this with Jesus Christ. Christ as head is not remote from his church, simply telling it what to do. He and his body, the church, are spiritually one, they are integrally joined together. This is what is meant by union with Christ (Ephesians 1:3-14; note the words 'in Christ', 'in him'). This is a spiritual reality. It is true for each believer, but not in an individualistic way. The Holy Spirit, who joins the believer to Christ, also joins him or her to the church.

Both the whole church, and each local church, is under the control of its head, Jesus Christ. His mind is revealed to us in the Bible, and what is revealed is brought home to our hearts by the Holy Spirit. The Spirit also helps us to see how Jesus' words apply in our own particular situations. All local churches are under the same head and guided by the same Spirit. Though they have many of the same challenges and problems, yet there is something unique about every church. There are always some differences between churches.

You can see this clearly in Revelation chapters 2 and 3. The Lord Jesus has a message for each of the seven churches of Asia. These churches are all in the same area yet they are all different, their spiritual conditions are different; the words they need to hear are different. Christ speaks to the churches individually and only he truly knows what those churches need. He praises and he warns as he sees what is needed. But though he speaks to each church and reveals very different situations and needs, his final word is always this: 'He who has an ear, let him hear what the Spirit says to the churches.' In other words, what he says to one church will always prove to be helpful for the others, though this may not be for the present, but in future days.

This is why each church must listen and learn from Christ as he speaks to it through his Word. It is a mistake simply to copy other churches, but it is also foolish not to learn from what Christ says to them. We shall see later that this means, in particular, that the elders, or shepherds, of the church must give themselves to prayer and ministry of the word, just as the apostles did (Acts 6:4). That word is open to all, but it is the special duty of those who oversee the church to search the Scriptures and to consider the condition and needs of the church in the light of what the Scriptures say and to minister to the church accordingly.

We shall especially note three points about Jesus Christ being the Head of the church. Firstly, this means he loves the church. When Paul is speaking about husbands and wives in Ephesians 5 he says this: 'Husbands, love your wives, as Christ loved the church and gave himself up for her ... In the same way husbands should love their wives as their own bodies. He who loves his wife loves himself. For no one ever hated his own flesh, but nourishes and cherishes it, just as Christ does the church, because we are members of his body' (vv. 25,28-30).

Secondly, because the church and all its members are members of the body of Christ this means that wherever those members go and whatever they do, they are always necessarily linked to him. From one point of view this is wonderful; he is with his people all the time. But it also means that all our sins are also committed in union with him, and that is a fearful thought. In 1 Corinthians 6:15-17 Paul says: 'Do you not know that your bodies are members of Christ? Shall I then take the members of Christ and make them members of a prostitute? Never! Or do you not know that he who is joined to a prostitute becomes one body with her? For, as it is written, "The two will become one flesh." But he who is joined to the Lord becomes one spirit with him.' An understanding of our spiritual union with him should help to keep us from all sin and evil.

Thirdly, if Jesus is the head and his church the body then we can be sure that he will never abandon it or its individual members. It is true that down through the centuries, while his church has sometimes flourished, at other times it has been through very difficult times. But we can be sure that in the end the church will have grown to a great number which no one can number who will be made perfect in glory (Revelation 7:9,10). Sadly, he may not always be able to rely on us; but we can always rely on him. He will never leave us or forsake us.

The diversity of the members of the body
When we think about a body, we are thinking about something which consists of many parts, but is essentially one. We shall need to consider this in a little while. While the unity of the church is frequently stressed—though by no

means always lived out—the diversity of its members is often overlooked. This, however, is the main point of the longest passage in the Bible which speaks of the church as the body of Christ, 1 Corinthians 12. So this is where we are going to start.

Diversity is stressed early on: 'Now there are varieties of gifts, but the same Spirit; and there are varieties of service, but the same Lord; and there are varieties of activities, but it is the same God who empowers them all in everyone' (vv.4-6). There is only one Holy Spirit, and one Lord Jesus Christ, and one God the Father, but there are a whole variety of gifts, and forms of service and activities. And these gifts are given to different members of the church according to the will of the Spirit (v.11).

We see nine different gifts mentioned in verses 8-10; these are all shared out among the members. Verse 28 speaks of eight different sorts of persons who have been given a ministry and gifts to fulfil that ministry. Then Paul puts the questions: 'Are all apostles? Are all prophets? Are all teachers? Do all work miracles? Do all possess gifts of healing? Do all speak with tongues? Do all interpret?' (vv.29-30). And the answers are, 'No! No! No! No! No! No! No!' In the church people are different, and they have different gifts and perform different ministries. You will find the same emphasis in Romans 12:3-8.

It is true that some of the gifts and ministries mentioned in these passages belong specifically to the age before the New Testament was written[1] but the principle is absolutely clear. To underline the diversity of the members of the church Paul goes on to write in terms of the parts of the body. He lists

---

[1] Some Christians would disagree with this statement, but this book assumes that it is correct. It would be too big a diversion to try and explain why this is so.

the foot, the hand, the ear, the eye, the head and the feet (but interestingly, not the mouth!). He mentions hearing and smelling (vv.15-21). He says that there are many members, but only one body (v.20).

Christians are different, and intentionally so, in the purpose of God. Being different they act in different ways and so can serve in a whole variety of ministries. None of them should try to be what they are not, nor should any be despised because they do not have the gifts that others have. This is something which many churches are slow to recognise. In many churches there is pressure for members to conform to a type rather than considering their gifts and the service that they can render which is appropriate to them.

Paul goes further than this. In v.22 he says: '... the parts of the body that seem to be weaker are indispensable'. The eye is a very sensitive part of the body. You can tread on someone's foot and they might be annoyed, but it is doubtful if any real damage will be done. But even a gentle poke in the eye will be very painful, and may do real harm. People take greater care of the weaker parts of the body, especially as some of them are of great importance. The lesson for the church is obvious.

However, in the next verses Paul develops this thought in a slightly different direction: '... and on those parts of the body that we think less honourable we bestow the greater honour, and our unpresentable parts are treated with greater modesty, which our more presentable parts do not require. But God has so composed the body, giving greater honour to the part that lacked it, that there may be no division in the body, but that the members may have the same care for one another' (vv.23-25).

We consider some parts of the body to be less honourable than others, and other parts we consider 'unpresentable'. Yet these are parts that we take particular care over. These are the parts which are not appropriate to be on view, so we cover them over. However, generally speaking, we try to wear clothes that not only hide these parts, but which also go towards making our appearance as pleasing as possible. Doubtless Paul was thinking of the flowing robes which both men and women would usually wear in those days.

His point is this. What we do with our bodies should guide how we act towards some members of the church. We cover over the 'unpresentable' parts of our bodies so that the whole body is attractive and appropriately and modestly attired. So, when it comes to the church we should take care to ensure that we treat members who may not have the gifts and abilities of others with especial thoughtfulness. Some people may have problems and difficulties rather than gifts and abilities, so we are to treat them in such a way that the health and usefulness of the whole body is improved.

These sorts of people may be those who are unwell, they may be elderly, they may have been very badly treated in the past; they may seem to have very little, if anything, to offer to the church. But the church has much to offer to them. And the world outside, and the Head and Lord of the body himself, watches to see how the church cares—or doesn't care—for its 'weaker' and 'unpresentable' parts.

We should remember, at this point, that the church is the body of which Christ is the head. So the question is: how would we expect the head to react and act towards its members? The issue in this chapter is not the sins that members may fall into. The issue here concerns both the abilities that people have, and their disabilities. The abilities are to be encouraged, and opportunities given for them to be exercised. The disabilities are to be overcome if this is possible, otherwise those who have them are to be helped and treated in ways that help and encourage them and so improve the unity and testimony of the church. Every member of a church needs to understand the important truth this chapter conveys.

The unity of the body

What we have just considered indicates that the unity of the church is not going to be easily accomplished. Indeed, it will not be accomplished at all unless the members understand this passage—as well as other passages of course—and realise the importance of unity and the nature of the unity that is required.

A desire for unity must not be allowed to compromise diversity. Yet sometimes this seems to happen in some churches. Some churches seem to be made up of people who are very similar in outlook and sometimes even temperament. Or it may be that one church consists very largely of younger people, whereas another church may be almost entirely elderly. It is understandable that people of similar age, or outlook, or social standing are drawn together, but churches must be very careful here. It should be our allegiance to Jesus Christ and our love for those who love him which brings us together. And love to Christ and those who love him should overcome what otherwise might prove to be obstacles to unity.

1 Corinthians 12 gives us some indications of the way in which the body should maintain its unity. First of all, all the diversity which we find comes from God himself. Verse 7 sums it up like this: 'To each is given the manifestation of the Spirit for the common good.' All the variety of gifts and abilities are given, and, like the different parts of the human body, they have been given so that the body can work as it was intended to. We do not criticise our bodies because they are made up of very different parts. We can see that having arms and legs, eyes, nose and mouth, and all the other parts enables our bodies to be much more versatile than they would otherwise be. So it is with the church.

Secondly, we do not criticise one part of the body because it is unable to do what another part of the body can. We don't expect our eyes to be able to hear, nor do we expect to walk on our hands—though a few people may be able to do this in a limited way. So it is important to understand that some Christians will serve God in ways that others will not. Moreover, God himself puts people with different gifts into the same church: 'But as it is, God arranged the members in the body, each one of them, as he chose' (v.18). These include the 'weaker parts' and the 'unpresentable parts'. It is, therefore, a serious matter if there is mutual criticism. Those who minister the Word of God must be particularly careful at this point. It is one thing to encourage God's people to use all their gifts; it is quite another to find fault with them for not doing what they are not equipped to do.

Thirdly, we should note what Paul tells us in verses 24 to 26: 'But God has so composed the body, giving greater honour to the part that lacked it, that there may be no division in the body, but that the members may have the same care for one another. If one member suffers, all suffer together; if one member is honoured, all rejoice together.' While the members are diverse they have nevertheless been 'composed' by God into a body. So they all belong together, and that by divine appointment.

The members of the church then, though different, are all to care for one another. No one of them has every gift; there are none who do not need at times the care and understanding of their fellow members. In the church we have to work together because we are all limited as individuals. That is why God has united us together.

As parts of a body we should feel for one another. 'If one member suffers, all suffer together.' If you have a headache, that affects you as a whole. You don't say, 'My head aches, but the rest of me is all right'—the rest of you doesn't feel all right! The church is a body and must feel as a body does, and care as people do for their own bodies. Similarly, if a foot kicks a football which then goes into the goal, the whole body rejoices. If a son or daughter does very well at school or university, the parents rejoice together with their child. Families are like that, and so it should be in the church.

Fourthly, those who are very conscious that their gifts are limited must be careful not to feel that they have no part to play, indeed that they cannot really be part of the body at all. 'If the foot should say, "Because I am not a hand, I do not belong to the body," that would not make it any less a part of the body. And if the ear should say, "Because I am not an eye, I do not belong to the body," that would not make it any less a part of the body' (vv15,16).

The fact is there are people who do feel exactly as Paul expresses it here. Such people often will not join the membership of a church because they feel they have nothing to contribute. They may actually feel rather threatened by the strong and active Christians whom they see as setting an example that all the members should follow. So they sit on the sidelines feeling inadequate when they should be embraced and encouraged, and ministered to if that is what they need.

The bond of love

This chapter in 1 Corinthians leads straight into one of the most well-known parts of the Bible, chapter 13, the great chapter on Christian love. We can say that if the church is the body of Christ, love is the life-blood which circulates through every member and enables the church to be what it should be and to function in the way that it ought.

It is important to see how this chapter follows on from the previous one. The last verse of chapter 12 says: 'But earnestly desire the higher gifts. And I will show you a still more excellent way' (v.31). It is actually possible that the first half of this verse should be translated: 'But you are earnestly desiring the higher gifts',[2] as if at Corinth people all wanted to have the best gifts; which, in any case, is what the chapter seems to suggest. Paul's remedy for this is to show the Corinthians a far better way: the more excellent way of love.

He starts in the opening three verses by saying that even if a person was to have the greatest gifts imaginable, he would still be nothing if he lacked love. It is easy to agree with that in theory, but the fact is many of us do desire abilities that would bring us a reputation and boost our own self-esteem. We are told here that the greatest speakers, the greatest intellectuals, the greatest benefactors—such people are nothing; they are worthless if they do not have love.

So Paul begins to show us what love is like, what it does, and what it does not do. And he says this to show us how love will reveal itself in the fellowship of the church. If the very different members of the body of Christ are going to live and serve their Head together as they should, then they will need to live out in practice what Paul spells out in verses 4 to 8a.

His opening words are not surprising in this context: 'Love is patient and kind.' Older versions use the word 'longsuffering' rather than 'patient'. 'Longsuffering' is perhaps rather strong, but the word 'patient' has lost the idea of suffering altogether. We can all be patient in some circumstances; but Paul is anticipating the difficult situations that can arise where there are considerable differences in gifts and character. There are actually two verbs here, and their tense is continuous: 'Love goes on being patient and being kind.'

---

2 This alternative reading can be seen in the margin of NIV.

Of course, in addition to the diversity which we find in chapter 12, we have to remember that no Christian is perfect. All are sinners, and we are all capable of attitudes and behaviour which are not fitting for the followers of Christ. Elsewhere Paul has this also in mind when he writes: 'Let all bitterness and wrath and anger and clamour and slander be put away from you, along with all malice. Be kind to one another, tenderhearted, forgiving one another, as God in Christ forgave you. Therefore be imitators of God, as beloved children. And walk in love, as Christ loved us and gave himself up for us, a fragrant offering and sacrifice to God' (Ephesians 4:31–5:2).

And similarly in Colossians 3:12-14: 'Put on then, as God's chosen ones, holy and beloved, compassion, kindness, humility, meekness, and patience, bearing with one another and, if one has a complaint against another, forgiving each other; as the Lord has forgiven you, so you also must forgive. And above all these put on love, which binds everything together in perfect harmony.'

To return to 1 Corinthians 13 it is interesting that Paul also tells us what love does not do: '...love does not envy or boast; it is not arrogant or rude. It does not insist on its own way; it is not irritable or resentful; it does not rejoice at wrongdoing' (vv.4-6). Negatives are sometimes important, and if church life is going to be harmonious there are attitudes and actions for which there is no place. However, Paul returns to the positive as he concludes his description of love in practice. In this case I am quoting from J.B. Phillips' 'Letters to Young Churches' as I believe he has captured the sense of Paul's words in a helpful way: 'Love knows no limits to its endurance, no end to its trust, no fading of its hope; it can outlast anything. It is, in fact, the one thing that still stands when all else has fallen.'

It is not uncommon in these days to hear of people moving from one church to another in the same neighbourhood over something that has dissatisfied them. Nor is it uncommon to hear of churches which have divided over some issue or problem, resulting in two churches, perhaps not too far from each other. Or again, to come across Christians who have been members in a church, or perhaps churches, but now attend a new church, but will not become members. They have no desire any more to be a member anywhere; they have had enough of that! These things are very sad. The antidote to them is found in 1 Corinthians 12 and 13.

Chapter 4
The church and its ministers (1)

In this chapter and the next we shall look at those who are called to specific forms of ministry in the local church. There is, of course, an important sense in which all the members of a church minister in one way or another. For example, they are all to serve one another in love, as we have seen. Some may have some definite ministry to perform, such as teaching in the Sunday School. Christians also serve by their witness to Jesus Christ beyond the church.

However, in the New Testament we find that some were called to particular forms of service. It is to these that we turn our attention. Church life takes place in a setting in which some are given particular ministries, and it is important for all the members to recognise this. We need to discover who these are, what they do, and look at them in turn to see how they relate to church members and how church members are to relate to them.

At the beginning of his letter to the church at Philippi, Paul writes these words: 'Paul and Timothy, servants of Christ Jesus, To all the saints in Christ Jesus who are at Philippi, with the overseers and deacons' (1:1). He writes to the whole church, 'all the saints', but includes a reference to two groups within the church, the overseers and deacons.

Similarly, in his first letter to Timothy he refers again to the same two groups. He does this by discussing the sort of Christian character that is necessary for those who belong to each. He begins chapter 3 like this: 'The saying is trustworthy: If anyone aspires to the office of overseer, he desires a noble task.' He then sets out those things that need to be true for a man to be set apart as an overseer. In verse 8 he begins another section: 'Deacons likewise must be dignified, not double-tongued, not addicted to much wine, not greedy for dishonest gain.' Clearly Paul expected churches to have both overseers and deacons.

With this in mind it is helpful to turn back to the Acts of the Apostles. In chapter 6 we read this: 'Now in these days when the disciples were increasing in number, a complaint by the Hellenists arose against the Hebrews because their widows were being neglected in the daily distribution. And the twelve summoned the full number of the disciples and said, "It is not right that we should give up preaching the word of God to serve tables. Therefore, brothers, pick out from among you seven men of good repute, full of the Spirit and of wisdom, whom we will appoint to this duty. But we will devote ourselves to prayer and to the ministry of the word." And what they said pleased the whole gathering, and they chose Stephen, a man full of faith and of the Holy Spirit, and Philip, and Prochorus, and Nicanor, and Timon, and Parmenas, and Nicolaus, a proselyte of Antioch. These they set before the apostles, and they prayed and laid their hands on them' (vv.1-6).

'The twelve' is a reference to the twelve apostles who were all in Jerusalem at that time. They had a ministry of prayer and preaching the word of God. These were their priority, and with the church growing rapidly they could not also attend to the practical needs of the widows. They had a spiritual ministry towards all in the church, and so seven other men were appointed to carry out the practical ministry which was necessary. This seems to indicate the beginning of two sorts of ministry within the church.

Overseers

In view of its use in the passages from Philippians and 1 Timothy we start with this word as we consider those who have a spiritual ministry in the church. Several other words are also used of those who have the spiritual oversight of the church. These are pastors or shepherds, teachers, elders, and leaders. These words are all important and help to build up a rounded picture of the role of oversight within a church. We shall look at each word in turn.

The word overseer was also used in a secular context at the time of the New Testament. It means supervisor, describing someone with a supervisory or organising role. However, we need to be careful. If we think of a supervisor in one context we might think of a position of power over others. But if we think of someone who has the task of looking after someone who is elderly or ill we would call him or her a carer. Our understanding of the word in this case would be very different. We are considering those who have the spiritual oversight or care of church members and it is crucial to remember this. There may need to be an exercise of authority where sin is concerned, but it is the all-round spiritual growth and welfare of the church that overseers are appointed to promote.

It is valuable to see what Hebrews 13:17 says about this: 'Obey your leaders and submit to them, for they are keeping watch over your souls, as those who will have to give an account. Let them do this with joy and not with groaning, for that would be of no advantage to you.' The verb 'keeping watch' is more literally 'keeping oneself awake'. It reminds us of the shepherds in Luke 2 who were 'out in the field, keeping watch over their flock by night' (v.8).

This will link with the use of the word 'shepherd' which we consider shortly. 'Keeping watch over your souls' is clearly of great importance. It might actually involve staying awake at night pondering on the needs of some of the members. The great concern of overseers is to promote and develop healthy spiritual lives in all the diverse members of the church. This is a very great responsibility. Titus 1:7-9 says: '... an overseer, as God's steward, must be above reproach. He must not be arrogant or quick-tempered or a drunkard or violent or greedy for gain, but hospitable, a lover of good, self-controlled, upright, holy, and disciplined. He must hold firm to the trustworthy word as taught, so that he may be able to give instruction in sound doctrine and also to rebuke those who contradict it.'

Overseers are accountable to Jesus Christ and this is very important. Church members sometimes think and act as if their leaders were responsible to them. There is a sense in which they are, as we shall see. However, much more important is the fact that those who oversee the church will have to give an account of their stewardship to the Lord of the church, Jesus Christ. Both overseers and church members need to keep this firmly in mind. In the end, of course, we are all answerable to Christ—how we have ministered if overseers, how we have responded to ministry if we are members.

Pastors or shepherds

Both words are used here because while the word in the New Testament is actually 'shepherd', the Latin word 'pastor' was used in some translations. As a result it became customary for churches to speak of their 'pastor', often without any realisation of what the word actually meant. This is unfortunate for a proper understanding of the role. The word 'shepherd' will generally be used in this book.

A shepherd is obviously someone who cares for sheep. Of course, we need to think of shepherds in the land of Israel at the time when the New Testament was being written. While it is true that shepherding is still similar in a number of ways, there are differences. The Eastern shepherd led his sheep to places where there was suitable pasture and they could graze safely. He made sure that they had adequate food and water. He needed to keep his eye on them at all times in case any wandered off, or they were threatened by a wild animal that could harm them.

The shepherd needed to see that they were safe at night time. Generally this meant putting them into a sheepfold and lying down across the entrance. He would go out and recover any that got lost. Doubtless when they were lambing he would take special care of them, just as happens today. He did not drive the sheep or use dogs to round them up; he went before them, leading them. He knew them all by name, could call them individually, and got to know their own individual characteristics and tendencies.

The last sentence reminds us that the work of a pastor/ shepherd has generally been understood to include visiting the members of the church in their homes in order to get to know them personally. This is very important, and can be easily overlooked. This is not just a matter of going to see those who are ill or elderly; it includes this but goes beyond it. All the sheep are the shepherds' responsibility.

If 'shepherds' only visit people who are in special need or in trouble, then others will feel threatened if a pastor makes a call. If, however, general visiting is understood to be part of his normal work then the situation is quite different. Ideally, such visits should be welcomed and time given for the family to gather, at least for enough time for there to be a short reading from the Bible and prayer. This is more difficult in these days, but if it is recognised as a normal part of church life and visits are made sensitively and arranged beforehand families will be glad to welcome a pastor.

It is helpful to read some of the Bible passages that speak of shepherds and sheep, as for example: Psalm 23, Matthew 18:10-14 and John 10:1-30. Matthew 9:35-36 says: 'And Jesus went throughout all the cities and villages, teaching in their synagogues and proclaiming the gospel of the kingdom and healing every disease and every affliction. When he saw the crowds, he had compassion for them, because they were harassed and helpless, like sheep without a shepherd.' This reminds us first of all that Jesus himself is the good shepherd; all other shepherds are simply under-shepherds. They are responsible to him, and encourage their flocks to trust and follow Jesus Christ. No shepherd today should put himself in the place that Jesus must have in the hearts of all believers.

Secondly, under-shepherds must themselves follow Jesus. They need the same sort of compassion that he showed. People today are still 'harassed and helpless'. When they turn to Jesus they should also come under the loving, thoughtful care of a shepherd (or shepherds) in the church. Such a shepherd needs to be someone who understands by experience the many and various needs of the human heart and who has learnt how to minister to these.

Another very important passage is 1 Peter 5:1-4: 'So I exhort the elders among you, as a fellow elder and a witness of the sufferings of Christ, as well as a partaker in the glory that is going to be revealed: shepherd the flock of God that is among you, exercising oversight, not under compulsion, but willingly, as God would have you; not for shameful gain, but eagerly; not domineering over those in your charge, but being examples to the flock. And when the chief Shepherd appears, you will receive the unfading crown of glory.'

This is probably the most important passage on the role of the spiritual shepherd. It contains both negatives and positives. Peter speaks as one who is himself a shepherd, one who knows both its temptations and priorities. The genuine shepherd, knowing what God wants for him, willingly and eagerly sets an example of Christian life and service which everyone can safely follow.

It is important to underline the last of Peter's negatives: 'not domineering over those in your charge'. It is easy to think of oversight as involving power and authority over the flock, and the human heart too easily wants to get its own way and exercise its authority over others. Peter's words remind us that Jesus did not say to his disciples, 'Do what I tell you', but, 'Follow me.' To a large extent true shepherding is setting a consistent and clear example of godly living which gives force to the words which are spoken.

This means that church life for the 'sheep' includes seeking to emulate the priorities of faith and behaviour which they hear from and see in those who are shepherds in the church. Of course the members of the church will have a variety of employments and interests, but it is the spiritual principles that they see in their leaders which they are to follow in their day to day living.

One thing that shepherds never want to happen is to lose any of their flock, even a single sheep (see Matthew 18:12-14; John 17:12). Shepherds do all they can to avoid this, and they search for a sheep when it wanders away and gets lost. Spiritual shepherds need the same heart and mindset. Some who appear to be believers may wander from the church, and this will grieve the shepherd, even though he has done all he could in the circumstances.

Teachers

In Ephesians 4:11,12 we read: 'And he gave the apostles, the prophets, the evangelists, the pastors and teachers, to equip the saints for the work of ministry, for building up the body of Christ.'[3] Apostles and prophets belonged to the beginning of the church, as already noted. Evangelists will be considered later on in this book. Our concern here is with 'pastors and teachers'. We shall not spend time here considering whether these may be two groups of people. Many writers believe that the words mean something like, 'those who shepherd by teaching', and this is how we understand it here.

We have already seen that Titus includes 'instruction in sound doctrine' as part of the responsibility of an overseer and that the apostles in Acts 6 devoted themselves to prayer and the ministry of the word. This must mean that unless a man has some ability to teach others he cannot be considered for the role of overseer. However, being a Christian teacher is not simply a matter of human ability or the gift of speaking in an interesting way, though clearly God can use such gifts. The Word of God is not just a message to be taught. It needs to be a living force in the heart and life of the one who teaches it. As Paul said: 'Since we have the same spirit of faith according to what has been written,

---

3   This is the rending of the ESV. Older version would include a comma after 'saints'. This would indicate that Christ has given gifted people for three purposes: to equip the saints, for the work of ministry, and for building up the body of Christ. The more modern rendering means that it is the saints who carry out the work of ministry. It is difficult to be sure about the actual meaning; I think the older is more likely to be correct.

"I believed, and so I spoke," we also believe, and so we also speak' (2 Corinthians 4:13).

Christian teaching must be based on and spring out of the Word of God, that is, the Bible. It is teaching that brings out all that God has revealed to us in the Old and New Testaments. This must be in the way that the Bible presents truth, not making some truths more important at the expense of others. It is also necessary to remember that teaching is not just a matter of preaching from a pulpit, needful though that is. Teaching can also be given on a personal level and it is a great blessing if a man is able to get alongside people and give them useful words of wisdom in this way. More will be said about this a little later.

There is an important verse which both those who aspire to be teachers and those who do not would do well to keep in mind: 'Not many of you should become teachers, my brothers, for you know that we who teach will be judged with greater strictness' (James 3:1). Teachers need to be careful that they are faithful to the Word of God; members of the church need to pray for them.

Elders

Elder is another word which is frequently used; we have already seen it in 1 Peter 5:1. We often read of elders in the Bible. The word was used in Israel, both in Old Testament times and New Testament. It was also used in secular Greek society. So far as its use in the church is concerned it indicates several things. While it does not absolutely refer to age, it does have the sense of maturity and experience, and the wisdom and authority that these bring. It is a word which speaks of someone who knows what life is like and who is therefore able to make mature and wise judgements. Jesus was thirty years old when he began his ministry, the same age as the priests and Levites when they began theirs (Numbers 4:23,30,35).

This means that those in oversight are likely to be men who are at least approaching middle age. However, younger men do sometimes show considerable ability and wisdom; some seem to grow up early. It is particularly valuable if these can be brought into a leadership which already includes older and more experienced men.

It is important to realise that what we are considering is spiritual maturity and understanding life from a spiritual perspective. Those who have great experience of business, or working with people, or who get on well with others, are not necessarily suitable for eldership. Churches have sometimes found this out to their cost.

Leaders

This word is used in Hebrews 13. 'Remember your leaders, those who spoke to you the word of God. Consider the outcome of their way of life, and imitate their faith' (v.7). 'Obey your leaders and submit to them, for they are keeping watch over your souls, as those who will have to give an account. Let them do this with joy and not with groaning, for that would be of no advantage to you' (v.17).

It is clear that the word 'leader' here refers to the same men whom we have already been considering, those who are elders, having the oversight of the church. Verse 7 emphasizes the fact that it is their way of life and their faith that are of first importance. These are worthy of imitation by the church members. Leaders are to be people whose lives mirror the life of Jesus Christ to such a degree that they become examples who can be safely followed.

It is also because of this that they are to be obeyed. As we have already seen, the picture is that of the shepherd. The shepherd is concerned to keep the sheep together and to guide them safely. Sheep, however, have a tendency to stray and wander off from the way in which they are being led. It is often the same in the church. The members are to follow the example that their leaders set and receive and obey the teaching that they are given.

However, these words about obeying and submitting are written for the members. They are not intended to encourage leaders to take to themselves any authority that goes beyond the Word of God. There are some things that belong to the consciences of individual Christians. There are other matters that the church as a whole should decide. Ultimately all Christians are answerable to the Head of the church himself, Jesus Christ the Lord. Leaders are not to elevate themselves as lords over those who belong to God.

It is also important for those who are called to this ministry to consult together and work together. All serious issues in church life should be discussed by the elders together unless this is impossible and decisions or actions need to be taken quickly. Being called to this work does not give individuals the right to speak or act just as they choose.

Those who are overseers, shepherds, teachers and leaders are to rely on the grace and enabling of the great Shepherd of the sheep, Jesus Christ. They know that there is grace sufficient for them from him. They have a great promise given to them: 'Let the elders who rule well be considered worthy of double honour, especially those who labour in preaching and teaching. For the Scripture says, "You shall not muzzle an ox when it treads out the grain," and, "The labourer deserves his wages"' (1 Timothy 5:17-18).

There is a further matter that must be considered here. So far it has been assumed that those who oversee a church and shepherd the members will be men. This is not just a matter of chauvinism or prejudice. This is what 1 Timothy 3 says: 'The saying is trustworthy: If anyone aspires to the office of overseer, he desires a noble task. Therefore an overseer must be above reproach, the husband of one wife, sober-minded, self-controlled, respectable, hospitable, able to teach, not a drunkard, not violent but gentle, not quarrelsome, not a lover of money. He must manage his own household well, with all dignity keeping his children submissive, for if someone does not know how to manage his own household, how will he care for God's church?' (vv.1-5).

Paul says that an overseer must be the husband of one wife. The emphasis is on 'one', only one wife if he is married, as most men would have been then, though Paul himself was an exception. Paul's words rule out the possibility of a woman being an overseer and other references support this (see 1 Corinthians 14:34,35; 1 Timothy 2:11,12). That Jesus chose men as his disciples, the ones to whom he gave the great commission in Matthew 28:16-20, is also very significant. It is also the husband who is the head of the home (see Ephesians 5:22-33) and who is to manage the household, taking the burden of responsibility (see *Christian Marriage* by the author).

However, we need to be careful at the present day how we understand this and explain it. It is not simply that eldership is open to men, but not to women. In fact, only a small minority of Christian men are called to this responsibility; men are not suitable only because they are male. Nor does this indicate that women do not have the gifts and abilities that men, or some men, have. There are many women gifted in many different ways as Christians. A pastor may well have a wife who is more highly gifted than he is. The Bible may not spell out fully all the reasons why eldership is male; it does tell us that this is so, and that should be enough.

Practical matters

What we go on to consider now is of special importance because the whole church is involved. The relationship between leaders and members is obviously crucial. When there is a breakdown of harmony, when there is misunderstanding or mistrust between the members and their leaders, then the church is in a serious condition. The glory of God and his blessing on his people are both put at risk.

In many churches that practised believers' baptism the situation in the past tended to be like this. Each church had a pastor, generally full-time, and there was also a group of deacons with whom he met on a regular basis [deacons will be considered in the next chapter]. While this often worked reasonably well it is not what the Bible indicates should be the case. In many churches now the situation is very different.

The practice now is often for there to be a pastor and alongside him several other men who have been appointed as elders; though not in small churches which do not have such men available. The pastor is most usually called from outside the church, while the other elders are usually appointed from within the church. In both cases these men will be called by the church members.

In all Independent churches—that is, churches which look to Jesus Christ through his Word for his guidance and direction—it is the members who choose the elders. This is implied by the Bible, rather than explicitly stated. In Acts 14 we read of Paul and Barnabas returning to the churches they had planted to encourage and strengthen them. We are also told: 'And when they had appointed elders for them in every church, with prayer and fasting they committed them to the Lord in whom they had believed' (v.23).

In a missionary situation like this Paul and Barnabas would naturally have led the service of appointment. However, we cannot imagine that they would have simply chosen the elders and imposed them. During the period that they had been away some of the converts would naturally have begun to demonstrate those qualities which Paul would later set out in 1 Timothy 3:1-7. It would have been such men who were appointed.

In the last verse of that passage we read of an overseer: 'Moreover, he must be well thought of by outsiders, so that he may not fall into disgrace, into a snare of the devil.' If a person must have a good reputation among outsiders before he can become an elder, he must surely also have gained a similar reputation among members who would know him even better. Ultimately it is Jesus Christ who calls an elder through the church. He does this in answer to the prayers of the people, and as they assess the gifts of a man in the light of what the Word of God says.

The point that must be emphasized is that choosing a man to be a pastor/elder is a serious responsibility. All members need to realise that they must avoid jumping to conclusions without thinking things through carefully. They need to pray, to evaluate the gifts of a man in the light of Scripture and to think carefully about the situation and need of the church. They need to be able to have conscientious reasons for their decision. Not necessarily because they will be asked for them by the church or need to make them known. Rather, because they are responsible to the head of the church, Jesus Christ.

The nature of eldership

If the church is the body that calls elders to serve, what should they be looking for in those who are suitable for such service? You will often find that the passage in 1 Timothy 3:1-7 is headed in the Bible, 'Qualifications for eldership', or words to that effect. This seems to be a mistake. The vital truth that is emphasized in that passage is that is it only men whose godliness is clearly seen who should be considered.

Those who teach the Word of God in the church must not only be good speakers, but know how to understand, explain and apply that Word. Generally, a clear distinction is made in church members' minds between the pastor and other elders. This cannot be justified by Scripture. Some distinctions may be made as we shall see later, but Scripture gives no grounds for different levels of eldership.

It needs to be understood that eldership is a full-time calling, at least in principle. This is clear from Acts 6:4; 1 Timothy 5:17,18, and 1 Timothy 4:13 also implies the same. Shepherding a flock is not a spare time occupation. Does this mean that all elders should be paid by the congregation? Not necessarily; Paul was a zealous evangelist and missionary, but he was prepared, when it seemed right, to earn his own living by tent-making (see Acts 18:1-3).

To put things into modern language, eldership is the career of those who are called to it. It is their primary responsibility; in ideal circumstances they would earn their living that way. But churches may not be able to afford to support more than one man full time; some may not be able to support even one. Eldership can never be simply a 'hobby' for the gifted and energetic, but an elder may work sufficiently to support himself and his family if there is need for this.

This leads us to consider why there may need to be several elders and what they actually do. Firstly, it is unlikely for one man to have all the gifts needed for the oversight of a church. Secondly, some churches may have numbers of people with difficult problems; and, thirdly, once church membership is reaching towards a hundred, one man is likely to struggle to care for them all.

When considering elders it is a mistake to look for men with identical gifts. Clearly there must be one, at least, who can preach the Word of God effectively; that is very important. However, not every good preacher is as effective in personal counselling nor in ministering both to the elderly and to younger people. So, in choosing elders, members should look for a variety of gifts if possible. An eldership should not consist of men who are much the same, but of spiritual men who each bring their own contribution. It is a team working together for the good of all and the glory of God.

At this point it is valuable to look at Acts 13:1-3: 'Now there were in the church at Antioch prophets and teachers, Barnabas, Simeon who was called Niger, Lucius of Cyrene, Manaen a member of the court of Herod the tetrarch, and Saul. While they were worshipping the Lord and fasting, the Holy Spirit said, "Set apart for me Barnabas and Saul for the work to which I have called them." Then after fasting and praying they laid their hands on them and sent them off.'

We notice firstly that there were both prophets and teachers, two different sorts of teaching appropriate to those days. Secondly, one of them is described as being 'a member of the court of Herod', which seems to indicate that he also had important secular functions to perform. Thirdly, they spent time together, in this case worshipping God with fasting.

Any such leadership needs to meet frequently and regularly; if possible once a week is best. Elders need to pray often to seek God's face and will together, and the church needs to know that this is happening. Generally speaking the main preacher will be the pastor and chair the elders meetings, in so far as a chairman may be needed. Elders' meetings should be regular and formal in one sense, and their tone should be that of men who are charged with a great task. They meet together in order to help one another to carry it out to the best of their ability and for the glory of God.

The teaching and pastoral care, therefore, comes out of a shared prayerfulness in which the interests, concerns and needs of the flock are regularly brought before the great Shepherd himself. It is also valuable if elders' meetings at times discuss theological and pastoral issues in general. The ministry to the people and pastoral care must also flow out of a deep understanding of biblical truth. Mere pragmatism and unthinkingly following current trends in other churches need to be avoided.

Qualifications for eldership

When it comes to qualifications, the church is to look for those who can fulfil the role that is needed. A man who is often going to preach the Word of God usually needs a thorough training, though this may not always be possible. It is better if he knows the original languages of the Bible, has a good understanding of how to interpret it and its main teachings. In particular, he ought to understand people's spiritual needs and be able to preach effectively to mind and heart.

It is helpful to consider the twelve disciples. They were trained by the Lord himself. It is likely that they were all tri-lingual, knowing Hebrew and Greek as well as the usual Aramaic. They were trained over a three year period and clearly spent quite a lot of time together with Jesus while separated from normal family life and work. They were very different men who were thrown together, went about together and sometimes were sent out two by two. They had a common purse; they lived and slept communally as they learned, directly and indirectly, from their Teacher. The nearest parallel to this is a college course taught not simply by academics, but by men of pastoral experience and wisdom.

Not everyone in a ministry team needs such an education. Nevertheless, an elder needs an above average understanding of Scripture, a good understanding of people and some study and knowledge of the particular area of service in which he will minister. Spiritual, mature men with experience of both the world and the church are the ones to whom the church can look for elders.

The Bible gives no indication that elders should be appointed for any particular length of time. Normally, an elder would continue in post as long as he is able to do so. Obviously circumstances may arise which mean that an elder will need to resign. Normally, a man would come to the decision to retire when he reached an age which made it difficult for him to maintain his ministry as he should. If he does not recognise that he has reached this position the church may need to point it out to him, though with wisdom and in love.

It is usually the case that one man is given the title of pastor and, as has already been mentioned, frequently he comes from outside the church. Very often such a pastor will move on after some years if he is invited to another church. Pastors often consider that they are the only ones who need to decide whether or not to move on. However, a pastor was called by Christ through the church and, if he judges rightly, he will consider that this call came after the church had prayed and sought the mind of the Lord as far as they could be expected to. This should mean that he will at least consult with the church who called him before he leaves it. In the last analysis he has to act as he believes right before the Lord, but what his current church says to him should form part of the decision-making process.

One other matter may be mentioned. There is sometimes a discussion about whether there should be parity of elders, that is, are they all equal? It is, however, a serious mistake to think in those terms. All are elders, so they have all been recognised and appointed by the church. Nevertheless, if their gifts are different their functions will differ in some measure, and some will have much more experience than others, with one, or possibly more full-time, and others with some other employment. In these circumstances it is not wise to talk in terms of equality.

A pastoral emphasis

Elders need to remember the importance of the pastoral nature of their work. They generally read much more widely than church members, they discuss together, they are aware of trends in churches around them. They may believe it would be good to take on some new work or go in a new direction as a church. They are leaders, but only if they have followers! It is right for them to bring new—or indeed old—ideas to the church, but not to force them upon the members. A flock needs to move together, and the eastern shepherd did not employ sheepdogs for that purpose.

In the second half of his book 'The Pilgrim's Progress', John Bunyan introduces a character called Feeblemind, who says he will not be able go along with the group, which really pictures the church which was led by Greatheart. 'But, brother, said Mr Greatheart, I have it in commission to comfort the feebleminded, and to support the weak. You must needs go along with us; we will wait for you; we will lend you our help; we will deny ourselves of some things, both opinionative and practical, for your sake; we will not enter into doubtful disputations before you; *we will be made all things to you, rather than you shall be left behind.*' There speaks a true shepherd of the Lord's people!

Chapter 5
The church and its ministers (2)

Deacons

We have already noted the main passages which speak of deacons. A description of their characteristics is given in 1 Timothy 3:8-13 and it is generally believed that the seven men who were appointed in Acts 6 to care for the needs of widows were the first deacons. The word 'deacon', however, is just the Greek word turned into English but not translated. So what does it mean? The word 'servant' in the sense of 'one who serves others' is the most accurate: but this is not suitable in the modern day. Another word would be 'minister', but that would be confusing, as this is often used of a pastor.

So it is probably best to continue to use the word 'deacon', as this has gained wide usage. However, the important thing is to understand what deacons are actually supposed to do. In Acts 6 we see that they were concerned to make sure that needy widows received the help they required, probably both in terms of food and finance. It was the deacons' responsibility to see that widows were provided for.

Some have taken this to mean that deacons are always those who help in practical, rather than spiritual, ways. However, 1 Timothy 3:13 seems to suggest a wider role than this: 'For those who serve well as deacons gain a good standing for themselves and also great confidence in the faith that is in Christ Jesus.' It is surely likely that those who cared for the material needs of the widows would also encourage and help them spiritually where this was needed. Those appointed as deacons needed to be 'of good repute, full of the Spirit and of wisdom' (Acts 6:3).

We can note in passing that in some Episcopal Churches a deacon is someone who is more like a pastoral assistant. It can be the first step towards becoming a priest. There is, however, no indication of this in the New Testament; though of course it is perfectly possible for a man who serves as a deacon to be called later to pastoral service. The most we can say from the evidence is that deacons are those who have specific ministries within a church, but not the overall spiritual responsibility which belongs to those who shepherd God's people. These ministries could cover a wide spectrum of church life.

First of all it is useful to remember how deacons have often operated, at least in the United Kingdom. As has been mentioned earlier, in many independent Baptist churches the pattern used to be a pastor and a group of deacons. These latter were usually elected by the church and often their election was confirmed every few years at a church meeting. It was from the deacons that a secretary and a treasurer were usually appointed, but the other deacons often had no distinct ministries. Rather what they did was to meet regularly with the pastor, perhaps once a month and so formed a committee concerned with the running of the church. Deacons often continued for life and it would have seemed disrespectful for one to be asked to retire in old age.

This form of leadership often worked quite well, but it does not fit in with what is said in the Bible. The appointment of elders has altered leadership considerably, but the same basic idea for deacons has often continued so that deacons and elders meet together. These are sometimes called 'church officers' meetings, though the elders may also meet separately from time to time.

However, if a deacon is someone who is given a specific ministry in the church—as for example, treasurer or secretary, or Sunday school superintendent, or looking after the church building, or chief steward, or many other possibilities, depending on the size and nature of the church—then the picture is quite different. There is no particular need for all deacons to meet together regularly and even less for them to be regularly involved in joint meetings with the elders.

There is, of course, room for churches to do things in different ways depending on their size and circumstances. What can be said is that deacons should have some specific form of service in the church and that it is proper for them to cease this service when circumstances or age require it. It is also clear that there needs to be co-ordination between the different aspects of church life, and it is always important for the elders to ensure pastoral care and spiritual help for everyone in the church.

There is one very noticeable difference in 1 Timothy 3 between what is said about overseers and that about deacons. This comes in verse 11: 'Their wives likewise must be dignified, not slanderers, but sober-minded, faithful in all things.' The translation, however, is misleading. Literally it is: 'Wives likewise...', but the word could equally be translated: 'Women likewise...' If this latter is correct it would indicate that some deacons could be women, which differs from what we have seen for overseers.

The case for this understanding is strengthened by Romans 16:1-2: 'I commend to you our sister Phoebe, a servant of the church at Cenchreae, that you may welcome her in the

Lord in a way worthy of the saints, and help her in whatever she may need from you, for she has been a patron of many and of myself as well.' The word translated 'servant' here is the same word as that translated 'deacon' in 1 Timothy. Moreover the word 'patron', sometimes translated 'helper', is unusual. W. E. Vine says of it: 'It is a word of dignity, evidently chosen instead of others which might have been used.' It had a more technical meaning both among Greeks and Jews, which might indicate a particular church-given responsibility.

So the question arises as to whether, unlike overseers, there can be women deacons. It is difficult to be sure as the next verse in 1 Timothy says: 'Let deacons each be the husband of one wife, managing their children and their own households well' (v.12). So while verse 11 by itself might indicate that this is so, this next verse looks as if the correct translation in v.11 could well be 'wives'. However, if this is the case, it is strange that the same thing is not said of the wives of overseers. After all, overseers have a more definite spiritual role to fulfil and we would therefore certainly expect that their wives would need to be 'dignified, not slanderers, but sober-minded, faithful in all things'.

There is one other quite different consideration. If this is a reference to women, then it does provide a clear category for women who serve in various ways in a church. In the last years of the 19th century some Baptist churches in Great Britain began to employ deaconesses. These usually had some training as nurses and were involved in social work, as well as evangelistic ministry among women. They wore a distinctive uniform and, for example, proved very valuable in deprived areas and during the Second World War in London. There have always been women who have contributed greatly to church life and there is certainly a need for those who can counsel women with very personal problems, especially those which result from sexual abuse.[4]

Churches will have to come to their own conclusion about the meaning of 1 Timothy 3:11. It does seem better, however, if women are going to be employed in church life for them to come under a clear biblical category like 'deacon' rather than a title such as 'women's worker' which has no definite meaning.

We should notice that 1 Timothy 3:10 says of deacons: 'let them also be tested first; then let them serve as deacons if they prove themselves blameless'. 'Being tested' would suggest that they were given various responsibilities in church life to see how they carried them out, before being officially approved as deacons. The emphasis is not so much on their ability here, but their faithfulness and integrity, they 'prove themselves blameless'.

We need also to remember that many people serve in various ways in a church without becoming 'deacons'. Perhaps, for example, it would be appropriate for the person in charge of some aspect of work to be a deacon, but not everyone who is involved. For example, a Sunday School 'superintendent' might be a deacon, but not a teacher, perhaps a 'chief steward' but not everyone who welcomes visitors at the door.

Evangelists

There are only three mentions of evangelists in the New Testament. In Acts 21:8 we read of Philip the evangelist.

---

4   In my experience as a pastor it took years for some women to tell me of past events of a very personal nature which had greatly troubled them for a very long time. In one pastorate there was a lady who had qualifications as a Christian counsellor and she was a great help to some women in the congregation. Through her I was made aware of things I would probably never have otherwise known, and so was able to pray and, where possible, seek to help.

Ephesians 4:11 tells us that the risen Jesus Christ has given evangelists to the church, and in 2 Timothy 4:5 Paul tells Timothy to do the work of an evangelist.

We can see from the word itself that an evangelist is a 'gospeller', that is someone who has the gift and ability of making the gospel known. Such a person then has a ministry primarily to unbelievers, seeking to win them to faith in Jesus Christ. Timothy appears to be a rather special case in that he was urged to remain in Ephesus by Paul to sort out difficulties which had obviously risen in the church there. Paul appears to be telling him that among all his other responsibilities he must not overlook doing the work of 'an evangelist'.

This might imply that he was himself an evangelist who was in danger of being sidetracked while dealing with false teaching and lack of leadership in the church. After all he had originally joined what might be called Paul's evangelistic team (Acts 16:1-3; 17:14,15; 18:5). Alternatively, it may simply be an encouragement for him, in a new situation, not to forget to do what an evangelist would do, that is, preach the gospel to the unconverted.

Ephesians 4:11 indicates that evangelists are different from 'pastors and teachers'. The English Standard Version translates like this: 'And he gave the apostles, the prophets, the evangelists, the shepherds and teachers...' The Authorized Version tried to bring out the emphasis of the definite article by translating 'and some evangelists, and some pastors and teachers'. It does seem clear from this wording that these ministries are different, and so by implication their gifts also. Evangelists are surely set aside to reach sinners with the gospel; pastors and teachers have the primary role of caring for the churches that come into being through the efforts of evangelists.

We should remember that the work of the evangelist is generally not an easy one. He is likely to suffer opposition and disappointments. He needs to belong to a church which will support him in prayer and possibly also financially, and where he can receive the encouragement of its shepherds. It is to them that he can speak about his opportunities and stresses and seek advice when this is necessary. An evangelist has the burdens that come from an unbelieving world, while elders carry the burdens that belong to the people of God. For this reason an evangelist would not normally also be an elder, nor an elder be an evangelist; there should be a division of labour and a division of caring for the mutual benefit of both.

It seems likely that the role of evangelist has been undervalued in recent days, at least in the West, even though there are several high profile evangelists who have rightly gained wide respect among churches. Experience seems to suggest that among young men who go to theological college there are numbers who have a heart and burden for evangelism. However, those intending to minister evangelistically in this country find that the opportunities are more or less limited to three: joining an evangelistic society, going it alone as an evangelist, or else becoming a pastor. In most cases the last of these seems the most obvious option. However, when such a man does enter the pastorate one of two alternatives often results. He may give himself primarily to evangelism and this frequently means that the pastoral needs of the members are neglected. Alternatively he gives himself to pastoral care. In this case he often has less and less time for evangelism and gradually he loses his evangelistic zeal. It is far better for an evangelist to belong to a church which supports him in his evangelistic enterprises, but does not limit his evangelistic usefulness by giving him other responsibilities in his church.

In recent years there has been far too much reliance on pastors trying to preach the gospel at services of worship. It is much better to look for those who have the particular gift and ability of presenting the gospel and setting them aside for that work. Churches do not now get large numbers of unbelievers in their services as they did in the past when 'going to church' was the thing to do on Sundays. Nor should we think of most church services as primarily evangelistic events; they are supremely the church's worship of its Lord. There is a great need to re-establish the role of evangelist and to link that more closely with the local church.

There has recently been an emphasis on church-planting though this has not always been as a result of the use of evangelists. What the apostle Paul and others clearly did in New Testament times was an evangelism that led to the birth and growth of a church in towns and cities where none existed. Today's church-planting, however, is not always the same as that of the apostles. Some church-planting in these days really means adding a church of a slightly different type or denomination in an area which already has churches. This is understandable if the churches concerned have clearly departed from New Testament teaching and practice, but not in other circumstances. In many towns and cities in Britain today new churches are constantly being started, sometimes only round the corner from other churches with slightly different doctrinal beliefs or practices. But that needs another book!

Missionaries

This heading has been included because the work of mission is very important. Although the word 'missionary' is not used in Scripture it is in common use among Christians and the relationship of missionaries to the local church is very important. Apparently the word itself originally came from the Roman Catholic mass. This concludes, in Latin of course, with the words 'Ite, missa est', which is usually translated, 'Go forth, the Mass is ended.' However, it is often given the sense of being sent out in the light of what Christ has accomplished, that is, to live and serve him amongst the rest of society. Whatever the exact origin of the words 'mission' and 'missionary' it is clearly based on the Latin original. Its meaning reminds us that all Christians are called to mission in the sense of serving and living for Christ at home, at work and amongst our friends and neighbours.

'Missionary' itself is a fairly recent name which actually covers a wide variety of callings. While it is more generally used to refer to those who go to other countries in some Christian work, it is also used of 'home missionaries'. It is difficult to know why we call some of these evangelists, but not others. However, while the term 'missionary' is used for those who serve as evangelists and pastors it also includes many other forms of Christian service, including doctors, nurses, teachers and so on, particularly when it refers to Christian work overseas.

Whether we are talking about 'missionaries' in our own country or those who go abroad, they will normally all belong to churches, and will usually be sent out from their churches. First of all, then, it is the responsibility of those who minister the Word in the churches to show the biblical need for those who will serve in mission, and to urge members to consider prayerfully and carefully what the Lord may be calling them to do.

There needs to be balance here. It is clear that marriage, family life and what we call secular employment should all be considered callings from God (see 1 Corinthians 7:17-24). All Christians should ask the Lord to guide their lives and recognise that in all the variety of employment and circumstances of life he is leading them on. At the same time it is right for Christians to search their hearts, to consider the gifts and abilities that they seem to have, and be ready for the Lord to guide them into new paths, and be open to the possibility of specific Christian work.

It is also the responsibility of pastors and preachers to give as clear guidance as they can from the Bible about every aspect of living as a Christian, so that must include the possibility of believers being called to Christian mission in this country or overseas. The needs both at home and abroad need to be clearly spelled out. There have been pastors who, while they have been called to their own ministries, have still had a great concern for the gospel in other parts of the world, and have been used to guide members of their congregations to that work.

Churches should continue to support those who become missionaries, wherever they may serve. Evangelists who travel round and take many different evangelistic events may come back to the home church tired out, and sometimes greatly discouraged. They need the prayers of their home church and the wise understanding and ministry of its elders. When missionaries go abroad, usually with long term service in view, they need the prayers of God's people while they are there. They will send prayer letters home, but it will be an encouragement if they receive letters in return from their friends. When they return, whether for furlough or because their service has come to a conclusion, they may suffer some reverse culture shock. They too will probably face a tiring time of travelling to many churches, often showing the same videos and saying much the same things. How glad they will be then for the love, understanding and support of faithful friends at home.

Sometimes missionaries—and ministers too—find they cannot cope with all the demands put on them; breakdowns in health are sometimes part of the cost of faithful service for Christ. Some will return to their home church for this reason. Be careful of condemnation in such cases. Loving, bur faithful, understanding and support is what is needed at such a time. This is all part of church life.

Widows

It may seem strange to have this heading, but at this point we look at 1 Timothy 5:3-16 and its implications. This passage is primarily about providing care for elderly widows who have no-one else to do this for them. Paul expects other family members who are believers to care for widows who are older, and he prefers that younger widows should remarry. Younger women might be in a position to look after themselves but the church needs to take care of those over the age of sixty. We should not think we need to follow exactly what Paul says here, it is the principle which is important.

He speaks about a list, that is, a definite group of widows who are supported by the church. However, when he describes the sort of widow he has in mind he says: 'She who is truly a widow, left all alone, has set her hope on God and continues in supplications and prayers night and day' (v.5). And later he adds: 'having a reputation for good works: if she has brought up children, has shown hospitality, has washed the feet of the saints, has cared for the afflicted, and has devoted herself to every good work' (v.10).

In other words while care is spoken of here, there is more to it than that. Here are women who have set a good example, who have been a blessing to the church and who continue in supplications and prayers. Two points can be noticed. The church has a special responsibility towards those whose lives have been an example of godliness and spirituality over the years. Secondly, those marked out on the list are continuing to set an example of prayerfulness and are a continuing reminder of the beauty of a true Christian life and Christian womanhood.

There may be no direct application of this passage today in many cases, but we must never forget our obligation to those in need. However, it is a reminder of the powerful testimony of godly lives and the great influence that believing women have in the life and spirituality of the church. The world might scoff at Paul's words, but they point to an important element in church life. While in some countries the authorities provide material care for the elderly, there is always an ongoing need for the church to care for their spiritual needs. Circumstances may arise where there is need for both.

Chapter 6
The church members meeting together

For most of the time the members of a church will be either at home or at work. There are responsibilities to fulfil in both locations. They are still God's people, of course, and will seek to live and act in ways that are consistent with their faith and so glorify God: 'So, whether you eat or drink, or whatever you do, do all to the glory of God' (1 Corinthians 10:31).

However, as God's people in the place where they live, they also need to come together. The letter to the Hebrews says: 'let us consider how to stir up one another to love and good works, not neglecting to meet together, as is the habit of some, but encouraging one another, and all the more as you see the Day drawing near' (10:24-25). There will be some members who may well find it difficult to 'meet together'. These may be older members who are housebound, those whose work takes them from home, and all are likely to have periods of illness. In New Testament days most people were servants of one sort or another and that must have sometimes made for difficulty in finding free time to 'get to church', as we say it now.

Difficulties may also arise because some people have no easy way of getting to the place where the church meets. These may be people with disabilities or older people or students or those who have no transport of their own. Fellowship and Christian love mean that those who are able to will help in bringing such people together. It is also worth pointing out that in the past and still in many rural areas of the world Christians will walk or cycle for long distances in order to meet with fellow believers.

While meeting together should be thought of as a duty— we ought to do it—yet it is much more a privilege and a blessing. Christians who may be alone through no fault of their own realise how much they miss because they cannot have fellowship with brothers and sisters in Christ. Before we consider what happens on those occasions when the church does come together, we should remember that Christian fellowship is not restricted to those occasions.

Christians who live in a particular area are likely to have opportunity to meet one another quite apart from specific church meetings. Christians are to pray for one another, but they are also to help one another when there is need. We live in days when contact with others is easier than it has ever been. Letters and the telephone are being replaced by email and social media enabling almost instant information and communication.

These should not, however, be allowed to take the place of visits to one another or personal conversation. In a large congregation people will tend to get to know well those of their own age group and background. This is only natural, but it is important for church members to try to get to know everyone—or as many as possible in large churches. Real Christian fellowship goes beyond formal or informal gatherings that are arranged by the church. It is a spontaneous desire to meet with those who are our brothers and sisters in the Lord.

The worship of the Lord's Day

The Father, Jesus tells us, seeks those who will worship him in spirit and in truth (John 4:23,24). It is clear that from the beginning the growing Christian communities began to set aside the day of resurrection, the first day of the week, as the Christian Sabbath, that is, the Christian day of rest. On the Lord's Day Christians would meet together for prayer and ministry of the Word of God (Acts 20:7; 1 Corinthians 16:1,2; Revelation 1:10). This practice has continued ever since amongst the vast majority of Christians.

More recently it has been suggested that the meetings on Sundays are really for fellowship and teaching, while worship should characterise the whole life of Christian people. This seems a false contrast, and it means that services are more about meeting with one another than meeting with God himself. Worshipping God seems to become a purely private thing that takes place when Christians read the Bible and pray by themselves.

Christians should certainly seek to glorify God in every area of life (1 Corinthians 10:31), but our minds and hearts cannot be focused directly on God when we are at work or busy in the home. However, the great blessing of worship together is that everyone can give their full attention to the praise of God and the Word of God.

In Old Testament days the people of God looked forward with anticipation to the feasts when Israel gathered at the temple (see, for example, Psalm 84). The book of Revelation speaks of everyone in heaven joining together in joyful worship: 'After this I looked, and behold, a great multitude that no one could number, from every nation, from all tribes and peoples and languages, standing before the throne and before the Lamb, clothed in white robes, with palm branches in their hands, and crying out with a loud voice, "Salvation belongs to our God who sits on the throne, and to the Lamb!" And all the angels were standing around the throne and around the elders and the four living creatures, and they fell on their faces before the throne and worshipped God, saying, "Amen! Blessing and glory and wisdom and thanksgiving and honour and power and might be to our God forever and ever! Amen'" (Revelation 7:9-12). In this period between the Old Testament and the Second Coming of Jesus it is the great joy and blessing of all Christians to enjoy a taste of their heavenly destiny when together they worship the Father in spirit and in truth.

Worship is a spiritual exercise and so it needs the help of the Holy Spirit if we are going to worship as we should. When we gather together we need to remember a verse like Ephesians 2:18: 'For through him [that is, Jesus Christ] we both have access in one Spirit to the Father'. 'We both' refers to Jews and Gentiles. In Christ, and in our worship, we are all the same; forgiven sinners who have access to come before God to praise his name and receive his blessing and guidance through his Word. Nationality does not count, nor the many other differences between human beings. In Christ Jesus we are all one, indwelt by the same Spirit, reconciled to the one Father God. Our worship is spiritual, God glorifying and builds us up together.

Over the centuries there have been variations in the way Christians have worshipped, though in the main these have not been great. One way of understanding Christian worship is to realise it is responsive. That is, God speaks to us in and by means of his Word and we respond to him by sung praise and prayer. This is a basic pattern which can be clearly seen in worship in every era and which emphasizes the fact that the focus is on the congregation together coming into the presence of God.

There is no need for this book to suggest any order of service; a variety of patterns can be followed and each church may work this out for itself. Nor does a church always have to follow exactly the same pattern each week. We can certainly say that the Bible should always be read, explained and applied. Prayer is essential and also sung praise. The whole church may join together to pray, perhaps using the Lord's Prayer, or when it confesses its faith. The whole congregation needs to participate actively by singing the praise of God. While a pastor will generally lead and preach, others may sometimes take part, but the emphasis should be on the congregation as a whole rather than individuals.

It is a great thing to draw near to the living and true God. We might try and make comparisons with having an audience with kings, queens or presidents, but such comparisons are wholly inadequate. The living God dwells in light unapproachable; he is the Maker and Sustainer of all things; he is holy love, great beyond all imagination, glorious above any human thought.

We are to worship in the beauty of holiness. This is only possible in and through Jesus Christ, our Saviour and Mediator. It is only acceptable when it is the outflow of hearts stirred and purified by the Spirit of holiness himself. Yet it is wonderfully possible by grace and is the greatest privilege and blessing that we can experience while still in this world. The worship of the Lord's Day can and should lift our hearts and direct our desires and lives for the whole of the rest of the week.

Because of all that God is, the attitude we bring to worship should be one of deep reverence combined with thankfulness and joy. We should be aware of the wonderful privilege that is ours. We should also realise that coming before God together strengthens and helps us all, we are one in our faith and one in our praises and prayers. We come as grateful children to our heavenly Father. We are God's family in the place where we live.

Just as a natural family meets together for special occasions and there is a sense of belonging and unity, so in a far greater sense the family of God meets together to worship. Moreover, when we worship on the Lord's Day we know that all over the world brothers and sisters in Christ are doing the same thing:

> The sun that bids us rest is waking
> Our brothers 'neath the western sky,
> And hour by hour fresh lips are making
> Your wondrous doings heard on high.[5]

The sermon

In Protestant, Reformed church services, whether Baptist or not, the sermon is of great importance. In the sermon the Word of God, the Bible, is explained and applied to the members of the congregation. This should mean that what God has said is being brought before the people to be received, believed, taken to heart and obeyed. At the same time, it must be acknowledged that it is being preached by a man who himself is fallible and who can misunderstand or even misrepresent what God has said. Thus those who listen must accept what the Bible says, but may sometimes disagree or suspend judgement on something the preacher says. Just as preachers need to learn how to preach, so hearers need to learn how to hear.

When the Bible is being read in a service it is not so important for the hearers to follow in their own Bible;

---

5 John Ellerton 1826-1893

hearing has a greater power than simply reading. However, it is the other way round when the sermon is being preached. Then it is most valuable to be able to look at the Bible and see how the preacher brings out the message from his text, especially if he is preaching from a passage rather than a verse.

Church members should listen thoughtfully, following all that the preacher says. In particular, they need to realise that through what is being said God himself is speaking to them. The message of one part of the Bible is being brought before them. They should receive it, and follow especially its application to their own hearts and needs. They are being provided with spiritual food which will nourish them during the coming week.

The apostle Paul says: 'the sacred writings ... are able to make you wise for salvation through faith in Christ Jesus. All Scripture is breathed out by God and profitable for teaching, for reproof, for correction, and for training in righteousness, that the man of God may be competent, equipped for every good work' (2 Timothy 3:15-17). Here five purposes of Scripture are set out: conversion, teaching, rebuke, correction and equipping for every good work.

Assuming that a person has been made wise for salvation the other purposes are all very important and it is through these ministries of the Word that Christians grow and develop in their faith. However, we should not think that Paul's list here exhausts the purposes of the Scriptures. We may need encouragement, or strengthening, or a greater love for God and dedication to him and his people. All these purposes, and many others, are accomplished gradually, week by week as the Bible is faithfully ministered.

What about the preacher himself? In most cases it is the pastor of the church who will preach at most services and he will gain in experience over the years. However, there are others who show sufficient gift to be able to preach on occasion. How should those who have this responsibility approach their task?

The preacher is not there to draw attention to himself; or to show off his gifts and abilities. He is a servant of the Word of God and he ministers to those who are before him. In most cases those who preach will know the great majority of people who are going to be in the church congregation. He must preach to them. Sometimes preachers give the impression that they are preaching to a completely different set of people than those before them. They may sometimes earnestly call on people to believe in Jesus Christ, when they know personally that everyone present has a made a credible profession of faith. Sometimes they may rebuke humble servants of God harshly, simply because they are upset at the apparent lack of conversions or what they see as lack of progress in the Christian life.

A preacher must be absolutely faithful to the passage of Scripture, whether short or long, that is his text. Preachers rightly use all the books they can to help them understand a passage correctly. It is best, however, to start with the Bible alone, though perhaps comparing several reliable versions. Seek to get a message from the Lord from the text itself. After that look at the commentaries, dictionaries and any other helps that are available. In most cases they will improve a sermon, but the sermon itself will have come from God through his Word.

Hearers also need to prepare their minds and hearts to receive God's Word. They need to be receptive but also to consider what is said in the light of the verse or passage on which it is based. They should also be ready for God to search their hearts and to accept truths that they may not have realised before if that is what the Bible is giving them. They need to be humble, to be ready to confess sin and to put into practice those things that are appropriate to their own lives and behaviour.

Singing the praises of God

In Old Testament days there was singing at the feasts that took place at the temple, but only a section of the Levites sang, not the people as a whole. These Levites were accompanied by another section from the same tribe who played various instruments (See, for example, 1 Chronicles 25). As far as we know the only worship other than the occasions when the people gathered at the temple was family worship in the home. The Levites were spread out through the land and it may have been their responsibility to teach the law of God. (See Malachi 2:1-9; it is not quite certain whether the teaching ministry was limited to the priests or included the rest of the Levites.)

It was probably during the exile in Babylon that God's people began to meet together in what became known as synagogue worship. 'Synagogue' comes from the Greek verb 'to gather' and simply refers to the place where the people gathered. On their return to the land of Israel synagogue worship became the norm each Sabbath for all pious Jews, including Jesus. The synagogue service was very simple, consisting of readings from the Old Testament, a message or sermon, prayers and the unaccompanied singing of Psalms.

The early Christians followed the same basic pattern. In due course the New Testament was added to the Old Testament and specifically Christian hymns were added to the singing of Psalms, though still unaccompanied. Musical accompaniment only started in a limited way after several hundred years, and amongst Baptists, only in the 19th century.

The New Testament says very little about Christians singing together. The two main references are Ephesians 5:18-20 and Colossians 3:16. In 1 Corinthians 14:15 Paul speaks of singing with his spirit, but also with his mind. The word 'mind' is significant and may explain why both Testaments are restrained in their references to singing in worship and especially to the use of instruments. 1 Corinthians 12:2 is a difficult verse. Gordon Fee translates it like this: 'When you were pagans, you were carried away, as you were continually being led about to mute idols.'[6] It is extremely likely that music was part of the stimuli that led to pagans being 'carried away' to their idols.

Israel in Old Testament days was surrounded by pagan nations whose religions included sexual excess and people working themselves up with music and dance. The Christian churches in their early days were also in a Greco-Roman culture with many cultic religions which similarly involved all sorts of strange rites and frenzies.

The worship of the living God has to be quite different from all that. While it is to come from grateful hearts, those hearts are grateful because the mind has been informed and stirred by the truth of God's grace. They have not been worked upon by artificial stimuli which simply stir the emotions. This is why God's people sing hymns full of truth expressing their hearts' response to his magnificent goodness. All should desire to be free to sing, any instrument should simply be a help to keep everyone in time together.

On other occasions the church may have meetings which include other forms of music, but when corporate worship is being directed toward the Lord himself all should sing with mind and heart to him. It is good to sing both older

---

6 Gordon D. Fee, *The First Epistle to the Corinthians*, The New International Commentary on the New Testament, Wm. B. Eerdmans Publishing Co., 1991; p.577.

hymns and more recent ones. To sing a Psalm is to sing what countless numbers of God's people have sung down through the ages and been blessed through the singing. To sing a new song is what the Psalms themselves tell us to do, and reminds us that we experience and can express the grace of God in the present.

The Lord's Supper

This was mentioned briefly in the first chapter as we considered the four priorities shown by the very early converts in Acts 2. That passage spoke of 'the breaking of bread', while the term 'The Lord's Supper' occurs in 1 Corinthians 11:20. This remembrance of Jesus' death is also sometimes called 'Holy Communion'; this is taken from 1 Corinthians 10:16, though the ESV uses the word 'participation' rather than 'communion'. Another biblical description is 'the Lord's Table', as in 1 Corinthians 10:21.

This section concerns the way in which the Lord's Supper is celebrated. What is so fascinating about Paul's discussion in 1 Corinthians 11 of the Lord's Supper is that he does not tell the church in Corinth how they should celebrate it, he simply reminds them of what Jesus did when he instituted it. The implication is that when Christians meet together for the Supper they simply follow what Jesus did. Along with 1 Corinthians 11, each Gospel gives its own account of that event.

Some general points may be mentioned first of all. While in most cases the Lord's Supper will be celebrated by local churches, the fact that it simply took place with the twelve disciples first of all suggests that it need not always be restricted to the local church as a whole. Jesus added it to the Passover meal and this was normally a family commemoration. Jesus' own mother was in Jerusalem at the time but neither she, nor any other of the women who followed Jesus, were present with Jesus on this occasion. Jesus greatly desired to be with his intimate group of disciples to celebrate the Passover and inaugurate the Supper (Luke 22:15).

Secondly, although we cannot state precisely how often Christians in New Testament times celebrated the Lord's Supper, the implication is that this was done frequently. Acts 2:42 and 1 Corinthians 11:18-20,26 certainly suggest this. The Reformer John Calvin went so far as to say that no meeting of the church should be held without the four marks mentioned in Acts 2:42 being present. Churches have to come to their own decision about this. Once a week would not be too much, less than once a month would seem to be too little.

Thirdly, it is clear from Acts 2:42 that it is those who have believed and been baptised who should come to the Lord's Table. Feeling unworthy to take part is not a reason to stay away. We come to the table because we are all unworthy to come into the presence of God; it is the sacrifice of Christ that enables us to do so. When we feel unworthy, that is just when we need to see afresh what Christ has done for us. The Supper is not for 'worthy' people, but for forgiven and repenting sinners who must never forget the cost of their salvation.

There are two common ways of celebrating the Lord's Supper. Firstly, it is often added on at the end of one of an ordinary Sunday service, often with a short time between the two to allow some to leave the church building. The other way is to have an entirely separate short service for members and believers, perhaps on a Sunday afternoon.

The problem with the first of these is that it becomes an addition which is just tacked on and is often rather rushed. Before the Supper takes place some people will get up and leave and the pastor goes to greet them at the door. The link between the two services can easily be broken and the atmosphere of worship may often be lost. The second option adds another service altogether to the Lord's Day; and this often does not allow for more than a very brief word from Scripture to be given.

An alternative is for the Lord's Table to be an integral part of a service of worship with the whole service planned and kept within a reasonable time-frame. The difficulty here is that there are generally people who have not made any profession of faith in the congregation. Such people who attended regularly would not partake, but visitors might misunderstand or be offended. In the past some churches would give 'communion tokens' to its members and believing visitors; only those with such tokens would then take the bread and wine. However, very few people would understand that in these days.

When it comes to procedure it is natural for an elder to lead the service, though not essential. He would usually speak from a suitable passage from the Bible. Generally prayers of thanksgiving will be offered, first for what the bread signifies and then for what the wine signifies. In many churches the bread and wine are taken round to the people where they sit. Alternatively, members of the congregation may come forward to receive them. The latter is more suitable if there are people present who will not be partaking; they simply remain in their seats.

It is a sad thing that the Lord's Supper, which is of such importance and intended to be a great spiritual blessing to God's people, often seems rushed or simply a routine. Churches need to think through very carefully what their practice should be. The Lord's Supper needs to be central in church life. It unites the church around its once-crucified but risen Saviour. It keeps us humble, but fills us with thankfulness and assurance.

The Church Meeting

There are many meetings of the church, but what is often called 'The Church Meeting' is the occasion when its members gather together to consider the affairs of church life. It is sometimes called the 'business meeting', but it is the Lord's business which is its concern. While it may consider very ordinary matters connected with the building or money, all is done by the Lord's people for the Lord's work and must be carried out in a Christian spirit and for God's glory.

Just as Christians should prepare their hearts and minds for the worship services of the church, so they should prepare for the church meeting. All members should consider it their duty to be present unless circumstances prevent them from doing so. Some members may be afraid of disagreements or think they have nothing to contribute and so stay away. Sometimes this is understandable, as there may be difficult issues to discuss on occasion. Rather than staying away members should prepare their hearts with earnest prayer, considering thoughtfully and spiritually all the items to be raised, desiring that the Holy Spirit will lead the church to a common mind.

The leaders of the church, perhaps elders and deacons together, will prepare an agenda listing all the items that will be brought before the church at its meeting. It is right for all the members to be invited beforehand to suggest items that need to be discussed. In most cases these will be placed on the agenda, but sometimes the leaders will feel that an item is unsuitable or that the time is not appropriate for it. Members need to understand that the leaders know more than they do and so submit to their wisdom in this. It is never a good thing if a church meeting agenda is full of unexpected surprises.

It is unwise to allow items that are not on the agenda to be raised at the meeting. If there is something which seems of really pressing importance this should be communicated to the leaders before the meeting starts and left to their discretion. They can decide whether it needs to be raised, or may be just mentioned to prepare the members for a later meeting, or whether as leaders they need to discuss the matter among themselves before it comes to the church.

Church meetings need a chairman to take the church through the items on the agenda. Often the Pastor will lead the meeting, but this is not essential. It can be better to have an elder or deacon who knows how to chair meetings to do this, while the pastor can sit alongside and contribute when he needs to. The character of a church meeting must never be simply like a secular meeting. It needs to begin with prayer and a suitable word from Scripture; often a hymn will be sung as well.

It is helpful if the church leadership considers the agenda beforehand to see if there are any proposals that could be very controversial. If there are, then they can contact all the members personally. The same is true of all very important and sensitive matters. Otherwise what often happens is that someone raises a difficulty or objection; there is a stunned silence, no-else says anything and the person who has dared to speak feels quite isolated and wishes he or she had kept quiet. Then later on someone else tells that person that they agree but hadn't the courage to speak up—but no-one else knows that and, in particular, the elders are unaware that it is not just a matter of one, perhaps awkward, member.

If, however, the elders discover that going forward with a particular proposition is likely to be very divisive and cause unhappiness amongst the members then the best thing is for the matter to be dropped, at least for a while. A church needs to be united and go forward together. There is a right time to take difficult decisions, and there is a right time to delay. Very important decisions may need time for everyone to come to a proper measure of agreement.

It is always important for there to be good communication between members and leaders. One of the problems of church meetings is that some people do not feel confident about speaking up, while others can be very forceful in their views. Some people are very fluent and dogmatic; others are hesitant and stumble over words. Elders and deacons must be aware of this and ensure that, as far as possible, issues are discussed in a fair and balanced way.

How do members show what their desire is? In many churches decisions are taken by a show of hands and with most matters this is straightforward and causes no difficulty. In some cases some churches use a secret ballot; this is often the case with the election of elders or deacons. This is understandable and avoids any embarrassment; neither those elected, nor any not elected, know who voted for or against them.

Most churches will require a particular proportion of church members to be present at the meeting for it to take a decision. This is because it is very unlikely that every member will be able to attend all church meetings. Probably somewhere about two thirds of the membership will be considered suitable. When it comes to particular issues that are brought before the church very often these cause no problem. It would be possible to set a proportion of members at the meeting that must agree before adopting any particular item, but this is probably not wise. The fact is that it is generally better for this to be looked at pastorally. If it is a comparatively unimportant matter—say the colour the church kitchen is painted—then this can be a simple majority or even left to those who use it most.

However, if it is an important, but perhaps controversial matter, it is better not to go ahead even if it is only a small group who feel very strongly that this would be a real mistake. The matter need not be left there, though. The elders should then talk together with the group to try and understand their reasons for opposition. Sometimes those with strong views need to submit to the will of the majority; at other times their reasons may lead the church to take a better course of action. Ultimately, all church matters that are not a matter of scriptural obedience must be finally decided by the church and not simply by its leaders.

Chapter 7
Ordinary church life

Prayer

This chapter looks at church life in a more general way. It is concerned with the relationships believers have with each other and the more informal aspects of church life. It starts with prayer because this is so important in the personal lives of Christians as well as in the life of any church. If love is the 'lifeblood' of the church, then prayer is its 'lifeline', it is this that puts us in touch with our heavenly Father. Believers are to 'be constant in prayer' and to 'pray for one another' (Romans 12:12; James 5:16).

How believers pray for one another will depend to some extent on the number of members. In smaller churches it will be possible to pray for all the other members regularly. Some churches print out a list of members, grouping them under the days of the week or month. In this way all the members are reminded to pray for each other. In much larger churches it may be more realistic to pray in a general way for all the members, but to pray specifically for those who are known well and those with particular needs.

Christians often pray for members who are ill or who have problems, perhaps connected with work or finances. This is right and good, but it is more necessary to pray for each other's spiritual growth and usefulness. We desire good health, but growth in grace and likeness to Jesus Christ is more important. We should pray too for the personal witness of our brothers and sisters in Christ, including, of course, our own. We are to pray that their lives might reflect the fact that they belong to Jesus. And we should pray that they might be able to speak the right words when opportunities to explain their faith arise.

It is usually possible for church members who live reasonably close to one another to meet together to pray, at least on some occasions. This is sometimes arranged by the church or by members amongst themselves. A few people perhaps, or several groups, may gather once a week at a time convenient to them. These may be older members of the church, whose time is not restricted by employment. Others might be able to commit to short times of prayer with two or three other members.

Many churches these days have house groups which meet for Bible study, prayer and fellowship. These encourage fellowship at a more personal level than is possible when the whole church meets together. However, prayer meetings or fellowship groups should not be allowed to become occasions when people emphasize particular doctrines or express criticism of leaders or other members. Not everyone in a church will think exactly alike on every point of doctrine or practice and it is understandable for people who agree with each other to talk together. But forming particular pressure groups is unworthy of Christian fellowship.

Most churches have prayer meetings, occasions when people meet together specifically to pray. There may be an evening meeting in the week which is almost completely devoted to prayer. Churches often have a prayer meeting before the morning service of worship on the Lord's Day; sometimes before the evening service as well. It is understandable that not everyone who comes to a prayer meeting will pray. Some may never feel able to pray aloud. It is good and right, though, for most people to settle it in their minds and hearts that they are coming to pray. Long silences are not helpful. It is not a good thing if only a very few—usually the same few—pray in the meeting. If possible, come to a prayer meeting ready to pray at the earliest opportunity.

While prayer meetings should include praise and thanksgiving, this is not the main emphasis, at least not on most occasions. Sometimes it is right to have a meeting to give thanks specifically for some blessing or evidence of the Lord's goodness. However, we live in a troubled and sinful world. We ourselves are far from being the people that we ought to be. We know the needs of large numbers of our fellow citizens who are far from God. The main emphasis then for most of the time should be on intercession and earnest cries for the help and blessing of God.

Prayer should also be offered for the leaders of the church and for its various ministries. Pray for the worship of the Lord's Day and especially for the preaching of the Word of God. Pray that God would revive the churches by the power of his Spirit. Pray for the nation you belong to and its leaders. Pray for world mission, for the spread of the gospel to every nation, tribe and culture. Pray for Christians who suffer opposition and persecution as so many do in many parts of the world. Pray that God would keep them faithful, if necessary even to death, so that they may receive the crown of life (Revelation 2:10).

The church as a family

As we have seen earlier, a Christian church can be thought of as a family. Members are called brothers and sisters throughout the letters to the churches. What are families like? Families extend through the generations; there are grandparents, parents, children, uncles and aunts, and cousins. There are old and young, men and women, boys and girls, the nuclear family (as it is sometimes called) and the wider family; the elderly, the middle-aged, the young adults and the children. And that is just what a church is like too, except that the basic unity is spiritual rather than physical.

Let us start with the picture of marriage. A marriage is a wonderful event, but it has its difficulties too. It means an addition to two families, an addition to the bridegroom's family and to the bride's family. At the wedding it is possible that both bride and groom will meet members of the other's family that they have never seen before. It sometimes takes some time before the newly-weds feel really part of the other partner's family.

Some people are brought up in a church; their parents attend and from a very young age they attended too. When they believe in Jesus Christ it is usually not difficult for them to settle easily into the church as members. It is very different, however, for someone with no Christian background at all. Some are brought to faith in Christ having had scarcely any experience of attending church services, and may never have had close contact with believers before their conversion. In their case everything about the Christian life and church life is completely new.

This means that those who are long-standing members of a church must make a special effort to welcome such people; they must not expect such converts immediately to understand what many Christians take for granted. Members need to show Christian love, a readiness to help, but also to be humble and sensitive so as not to make any new member feel awkward. New members should be accepted as they are and allowed to learn and develop in their own time according to the grace of God at work in them.

Children in the church

Families are particularly concerned for their own children. They want them to grow up to be the best that they can be. This is true for Christian families and it must be true of the church family as well. However, a church cannot be concerned simply for the children of its members; it also desires to do what it can for children in the neighbourhood of the place where it meets.

For the children of members the most important thing a church can do is to help the parents to bring up their own children wisely and spiritually. Christian parents often need wise guidance and need to understand scriptural priorities. At the same time the church has to understand that while it should support and help parents as far as that is possible, yet God has given those children to the parents. It is they who have the ultimate responsibility; they need to feel helped and supported, but also free before God to fulfil their obligations as they believe Scripture is guiding them.

Churches generally have Sunday Schools for children and meetings during the week for children and young people. These have two main purposes: firstly, to teach basic facts and truths from the Bible; secondly, to show the need for turning to Jesus Christ in faith. If there are children who come from homes where the parents do not attend a church or make any profession of faith in Jesus Christ, then the teaching needs to be simple and evangelistic.

Parents, and churches, differ when it comes to whether children should be in the services of worship, in particular the morning service. Some churches provide childcare for very young children to allow parents to join in the worship. Some parents like their children to stay in the service even from quite a young age, but others may not. The church needs to be as flexible as it can to cater for families that attend.

Some churches have family services which aim to be suitable for children as well as adults. These can easily focus on the families that attend rather than on the Lord, so churches need to assess this possibility with care. True reverence and worship do not mean long prayers, difficult language and dullness. Children need to know that the whole family can draw near to God together. If the family has daily Bible reading and prayer together at home, then it is being prepared for the longer worship of the church.

In many churches morning worship has often included a talk for the children present in the congregation. This makes the children feel a part of the service even if they may go out later for a Bible talk of their own. A children's talk is not always easy for preachers, but it is good for them to try and communicate to younger people; older people, too, often appreciate a simple, straightforward talk as well! This can also be an opportunity for everyone to learn a simple catechism week by week.

We have to be realistic. After a service children can sometimes be a handful and can rush around all over the place. There can be difficulties all round. Parents want to be able to speak with their Christian friends, the children have been sitting still for what seems a long time, they want to play with other children; some might want to kick a football about.

These difficulties need to be anticipated and at least some basic guidelines drawn up. Some parts of the building— the pulpit, for example—might be out of bounds and members and their children know this. There might be a room where children can go to let off steam. From quite a young age children can be given jobs to do—collecting up hymn books, for example. However, the important thing is that this matter is considered by the whole church together and dealt with in a sensitive, pastoral manner. Parents are naturally upset if other members take it upon themselves to rebuke their children. Other members can be upset if parents seem to allow their children to do whatever they like. Such situations are pressure points which test the spirituality of a church and call for wise, spiritual handling by its shepherds.

Young people

Children grow up and it can seem that in no time babies in the church suddenly grow into teenagers, so new opportunities—and often new problems—arise. Many young people growing up in Christian homes come to faith in Jesus Christ during their teenage years, but it is also true that many find this a difficult time. The church needs to understand both of these realities.

It is important that undue pressure is not put on young people at this age to confess Jesus Christ as their Saviour. Some will react against this, while others may too easily make a decision which may not be a genuine expression of faith. In addition this period of life can be a time when teenagers experience considerable fluctuations of emotion and this can be very unsettling for them. At times they feel they are grown up and want to follow their own path, at other times they feel very vulnerable and may desire reassurance and yet feel too proud to ask for help.

While parents have the responsibility of caring for their children it is also true that those in their teens may often talk more to their peers than to their parents. This may be to others in a church young people's group, or it may be with school friends. Sometimes there are young people's leaders in a church to whom youngsters may go rather than their parents. All this can be difficult both for parents and for those who lead young people's work. Parents must try to keep as close to the children as they can, but they also have to realise that the process of growing up with young people beginning to take their own future into their hands, is often not easily accomplished.

All this is considerably complicated by the fact that in these days many children and young people are taught at school a great deal that contradicts or undermines Christian belief and conduct. The standards of behaviour and outlook on sexual matters of many of their contemporaries are far below what should be expected of Christians. These realities have to be understood and faced by parents and church members, by church and youth leaders.

So church members need to be aware of the problems and possibilities; it is too easy to be critical or to have unrealistic expectations. Prayer should be made both for parents and their teenagers. It is good to remember our own youthful days, both the struggles and the blessings we experienced. Remember too the circumstances of the young people. Some may come from homes that are far from sympathetic to the gospel. Some may suffer ridicule amongst their peers, at school or amongst others in the neighbourhood where they live.

Encourage as much as possible those who show signs of God's working in their lives. Try to be the sort of person that they will look to for advice. Make the effort to speak to them, not to cross-question, but to show genuine interest and willingness for friendship. Don't give the impression that you are always looking for something to criticise about modern life and modern young people. But be honest when there are things that genuinely distress you about contemporary life and behaviour. Explain why you feel as you do; this must not be simply because things are different from how they were in your day, but because they differ from the standards of the Bible and godly behaviour.

Very often the later teens are a time when young Christians begin to blossom and become enthusiastic in service and evangelism. They may take part in short-term missions or bring their friends to evangelistic events or services. This is a great joy to a church, which should thank God and be ready to give encouragement and guidance. It is true that young people will not always be wise and sometimes enthusiasm can run away with them. They may tend to think that older people are stuck in the past, and of course, sometimes they are right. However, if the church always seeks to give biblical reasons for the way it does things, it is a considerable help.

In many countries in the world now, young people go to college or university after leaving school, often leaving home to do so. The church should continue to pray for them and even if they have not professed conversion look upon this as still part of its responsibility. Many will get involved in Christian student groups and may be very busy in Christian work. However, sadly, after leaving the student world and settling down into the world of work and business, too many seem to lose their zeal and some give up church altogether.

There are doubtless a variety of reasons for this, but partly it may be that the church does not give enough teaching on the world of work and the pressures and problems of ordinary life. The Christian life is not just about being young and enthusiastic and everything being fresh and exciting. It is also about perseverance, about resisting temptation, enduring suffering while we keep trusting in God.

The elderly

Changes are taking place in many countries. With improved health care and social conditions people are living much longer than they did in the past, especially in the western world. So every church can expect an increase in elderly members who will also live longer than used to be the case. The education systems in some countries influence pupils against the Christian faith. This means that churches in those lands are likely to have more old people than those who are younger.

The Bible does not glorify either youth or old age. It does encourage respect for older people (Leviticus 19:32) and gives examples of those who have, in the words of Psalm 92:14, 'borne fruit in old age'. We may think, for example, of Joshua and Barzillai in the Old Testament, and Zechariah and Elisabeth, Simeon and Anna in the New. But the Bible is also realistic. Moses might have died at 120, 'his eye undimmed and his vigour unabated' (Deuteronomy 34:7), but he wrote: 'The years of our life are seventy, or even by reason of strength eighty; yet their span is but toil and trouble' (Psalm 90:10). Ecclesiastes 12:1-8 gives us a sad picture of the increasing weaknesses of old age before 'the silver cord is snapped' and 'the golden bowl is broken'. Some elderly Christians have to be compassionately borne with and cared for. To be 'with Christ' is 'far better', but the latter years may prove a hard coming to that glory.

It is important not to generalise. Older people have their differences as do those of any age. Some flourish as Christians late on in life; they may be remarkably vigorous and give good service in many different ways. But that is probably not true of the majority. Gradually they find their powers waning. The time comes when they may not be able to get out in the evenings. They are more prone to infections and seasonal diseases. As they grow older they are less and less able to meet with the church; and so spiritual help and encouragement needs to come to them. There are several problems that older people often face.

There may be feelings of guilt or disappointment as they find they cannot serve the Lord and the church as they used to. Sometimes they will try and force themselves to do things they are really not capable of doing, or doing adequately, and this makes it difficult for the church as well as frustrating for them. There can be a feeling of uselessness. To make up for this they may be told, 'You can always pray.' They may, however, actually find that because their minds tend to wander, prayer times can become more of a burden and distress rather than a joy and help. Older people sometimes lose a sense of assurance, especially if this has been rather dependent on their past activities. Those with a tendency to introspection are more often vulnerable to this, especially if they spend long hours on their own.

Older people often become more sensitive to all the things that go on in the world which they see or hear from the media. They become worried and tense, and have too much time to turn things over in their minds. They cannot shake off the impact of vile and evil acts on their minds as they used to. Hearing about wars and disasters, murders and sexual sins, upset and depress them greatly. Some aspects of life today distress those who were brought up in what seems now as almost a different age with a completely different outlook.

We live in days of great change. Change, of course, is a constant process, but the pace of change has increased considerably over the last decades and this is likely to continue. Older people, however, are not generally as flexible as those who are younger; they tend to get set in their ways. So it is not a good idea to have too many sudden changes in church life and procedures. Small changes that are shown to be necessary are best and these can be quite frequent.

In the church we should aim to overcome the youth/age divide which is too often found in the world. Older people can make valuable contributions to the life of a church. Rehoboam was to discover that old men can be wiser than young men (1 Kings 12). Paul was still writing wise letters in his old age (Philemon 9). Many prayer meetings consist largely of older people. Psalm 78:1-4 indicates that older people should pass on to the next generation 'the glorious deeds of the Lord'. Sadly, some older people can be repetitive and long-winded, so loving wisdom is required; many, however, may have stories to tell which illuminate the past and encourage the rest of the church to persevere.

The normal worship services need to provide for the whole church. Older Christians will often love hymns that have been a great blessing to them in the past. So aim for a balance of the old and the new. It is important for pastors to prepare the ministry of the Word of God with the whole congregation in mind. As they prepare they must visualise the people, young and old, think of their circumstances and needs, and try to prepare messages which will reach the hearts of everyone present. This means applying the words of Scripture to the practical lives and spiritual needs of the whole congregation. That church is blessed when week by week all the members of the congregation leave the worship services knowing that God has spoken to each of them from his Word.

Just as it is not helpful to think all young people are much the same, so with those who are older. Some have a wealth of Christian experience, some have had many trials and sorrows, some have always struggled with temptations that haven't bothered others, some are weak in body and perhaps in mind as well. Every person is an individual and must be treated as such. And, in a number of respects, older people are generally on a downward slope. They are growing physically weaker; they haven't the resilience they used to have, memory may be unreliable; they feel unable to do what they used to do or what they would like to do.

At the same time, older Christians bring a wealth of experience to a church. They have seen churches rise after a period of difficulty. They have proved the Lord's faithfulness over many years. They have often put up with discouragements and have learnt to look to the long term. Some are more vigorous than might be expected and 'still bear fruit in old age' (Psalm 92:14). In fact, all true believers go on serving the Lord in some respect almost up until the time that they are called home.

It is important to encourage old and young to mix, so that they can be mutually beneficial to each other. Older people are glad to be able to help the church as far as they can, and their contribution, even if it is small, should not be ignored. They should not be patronised. Church leaders, in particular, need to understand what older people can do and what they are no longer able to contribute.

The pastoral visitation of older members and attendees is important. It is also good if other members can drop in from time to time, and, where necessary, for churches to arrange for practical help. As we have seen the church is the family of Christ in a particular place; the members are all related by grace, all significant, sharing together the joys and sorrows, the stresses and blessings that belong to family life.

Those who are sick

Everyone is ill at some time and some people are particularly prone to poor health. Churches and their elders cannot be only concerned about the spiritual and moral health of members. Physical and mental health matter also. Moreover, ill health often has an effect on the spiritual lives of believers. Those who are frequently unwell, and those with some particular diseases often find this weakening and depressing; they need understanding and encouragement.

Some mistakenly believe that illness is usually the result of sin. It is true that people can bring illness upon them by foolish behaviour and God can use that to humble his people and draw them back to himself. Illness, however, is usually something that comes to believers just as it does to everyone. It never comes outside of God's purposes, but it is not generally a sign of his displeasure.

Similarly, some Christians seem to think that all mental health problems are the result of sin, or are the work of the devil. Again, however, this is seldom the case. It is true that the devil is always active and he does try to take advantage of our weaknesses. However, we can resist the devil, but we cannot simply resist all the pressures of life and the stresses and strains that can come upon us. We are fallen people in a fallen world and being Christians does not mean we will always be kept from accidents or illnesses. In fact, believers are often more sensitive and distressed than others by all the evils that they see in the world around.

It is natural for us to sympathise with those who are unwell; we all know, at least to some extent, what it is to feel ill and weak. Nevertheless, it is the case that some people have far less illness than others, and can fail to understand how others feel. It is also true that some make more than they should of their illness—sometimes this is a symptom of some other underlying problem to which they wish to draw attention. We need to try and understand one another, to bear with each other and give what moral or practical support we can.

James 5:16 has a sentence in it which is often quoted: 'The effective prayer of a righteous person has great power.'[7]

---

7   ESV margin

However, this actually comes as part of a section largely about illness in the church: 'Is any among you suffering? Let him pray... Is anyone among you sick? Let him call for the elders of the church, and let them pray over him, anointing him with oil in the name of the Lord. And the prayer of faith will save the one who is sick; and the Lord will raise him up. And if he has committed sins, he will be forgiven. Therefore confess your sins to one another and pray for one another, that you may be healed. The effective prayer of a righteous person has great power.'

One more matter may be mentioned at this point. Most churches attract people with various forms of mental health problems. Sometimes these people can be very demanding and even troublesome. However, they usually come because they have very few friends and they are seldom welcome anywhere else. They aren't usually church members, but nevertheless they should be welcomed and treated with thoughtfulness. However, leaders also need to be alert to the fact that some people may come who have motives or weaknesses that could lead to harm in the church.

Evangelism

This is a book which is primarily about relationships and responsibilities within the church. Moreover, evangelism is a large subject that needs a book on its own. However, there are some aspects of church life relating to evangelism that must be briefly considered.

Churches must always be concerned to bring the gospel of Jesus Christ to those who need to hear it and all the members must have this responsibility on their hearts. However, it is important to remember what we saw earlier about the way in which members of churches are gifted in different ways. Just as some Christians seem keen to get all young men in the church to preach, so there is often pressure put on nearly all members to engage in all the church's evangelistic enterprises. This needs thoughtful consideration.

It is the clear duty of Christians to pray for people to be converted, and every believer must also obey Peter's words: 'In your hearts honour Christ the Lord as holy, always being prepared to make a defence to anyone who asks you for a reason for the hope that is in you; yet do it with gentleness and respect' (1 Peter 3:15,16). More than that, Christians should look out for opportunities to bear witness to others. Though there is much that believers can, and should, learn about effective communication of the gospel, yet it is the spontaneous and natural testimony to Christ that is most effective.

When it comes to the various forms of outreach that churches may undertake it is important that people are not pressured nor automatically given responsibilities just because they volunteer. At the same time we should realise that some people have the gift of passing on the gospel in ways that very few others would be able to. These should be encouraged, but it would be wrong to use such people as role models for others. Leaders in the church should seek prayerfully to discover the gifts that people have and encourage them to use those gifts in the Lord's work, whether in evangelism or in other forms of service. Young Christians very often show a pleasing enthusiasm for serving Christ and leaders should guide and help them to discover those ways in which they can best do this.

It should be remembered that while evangelism is intended to further the cause of Christ it also has the potential to turn people away from the gospel. Even apologists of atheism do not expect Christians in personal, unplanned conversations always to be able to give a good reason for the hope that is in them. But if a church, or an individual Christian is engaging in some evangelistic activity the world has the right to expect at least a sincere, heartfelt, respectful testimony to gospel truth (see 1 Peter 3:15 again).

Handling disagreements

While all the members of a church should agree on the major truths revealed in the Bible and on the basic constitution of the church yet disagreements are bound to surface at times. In some situations people may well attend the church services, or may even be members, who would belong to a slightly different church if there was one for them in the area where they live. Many disagreements tend to be about the policy of the church on practical rather than doctrinal matters.

We should not underestimate the potential for disagreement and its consequences. In the very early days of the expansion of the Christian faith we find Paul and Barnabas disagreeing to such an extent that we read: 'And after some days Paul said to Barnabas, "Let us return and visit the brothers in every city where we have proclaimed the word of the Lord, and see how they are." Now Barnabas wanted to take with them John called Mark. But Paul thought best not to take with them one who had withdrawn from them in Pamphylia and had not gone with them to the work. And there arose a sharp disagreement, so that they separated from each other. Barnabas took Mark with him and sailed away to Cyprus. But Paul chose Silas and departed, having been commended by the brothers to the grace of the Lord. And he went through Syria and Cilicia, strengthening the churches' (Acts 15:36-41).

While this shows us how God over-ruled so that the result was that two mission fields were visited we cannot believe that such a sharp disagreement was honouring to God. The fact that God can bring good out of evil does not allow us to act as we please, nor be content with divisions that ought not to not take place.

In Ephesians 4:1-7 Paul writes: 'I therefore a prisoner for the Lord, urge you to walk in a manner worthy of the calling to which you have been called, with all humility and gentleness, with patience, bearing with one another in love, eager to maintain the unity of the Spirit in the bond of peace. There is one body and one Spirit—just as you were called to the one hope that belongs to your call—one Lord, one faith, one baptism, one God and Father of all, who is over all and through all and in all. But grace was given to each one of us according to the measure of Christ's gift.'

Similarly, in Philippians 2:1-5 he says: 'So if there is any encouragement in Christ, any comfort from love, any participation in the Spirit, any affection and sympathy, complete my joy by being of the same mind, having the same love, being in full accord and of one mind. Do nothing from rivalry or conceit, but in humility count others more significant than yourselves. Let each of you look not only to his own interests, but also to the interests of others. Have this mind among yourselves, which is yours in Christ.'

There are other similar passages that could be quoted but these two are sufficient to show us the love and basic agreement which ought to characterise Christian people. We are called to be gentle with one other, we are to be humble, we are to seek agreement and bear with one another in love even if we cannot agree together on every point. We are to be eager to maintain good relationships in the bond of peace. These are qualities that we have to develop and look after consciously and deliberately.

Disagreements may arise between two members, or perhaps two families in the church. There may be some different understanding of Scripture, some apparent problem in church life itself, or some problem whose cause lies entirely outside the church. It is all too easy for small disagreements to grow into serious divisions. Someone has been upset, but the person responsible doesn't think that he or she has said or done anything that needs apology, and so the separation gets worse.

If the original problem lies outside of the church, elders may allow time to see if those involved can put things right themselves. Indeed, this is generally the case with all disagreements; it is better for Christians to learn for themselves that they are responsible before God to live in love and harmony with their fellow believers. However, problems that arise within the church are generally more visible and can easily affect other members and so elders must be vigilant and wise. Once various friends start taking sides even a small matter can become a real hindrance to church fellowship.

It is possible for Christians to agree to disagree over a number of matters of belief or practice, but disagreements can easily lead to actual sin. Harsh words, a bitter or unforgiving spirit, exaggeration which virtually amounts to lying, these things are sinful and sometimes both sides in a dispute can be guilty of them. Sadly, these things are sometimes also found in a falling out between husband and wife, even among those who give every appearance of being real Christians.

It is not possible in a short book to go into any details of counselling or restoration after serious sins. This section is designed simply to alert all church members to the fact that none of us is perfect. We are all capable of reacting in ungodly ways or speaking a harsh word or avoiding those we don't really like or find it hard to get on with. We must listen to the voice of Christ as he speaks to us out of his word: 'A new commandment I give to you, that you love one another: just as I have loved you, you also are to love one another. By this all people will know that you are my disciples, if you have love for one another' (John 13:34-35).

When things go wrong

There will always be small disagreements and times when members fall out with each other but then forgive each other and put things right. Sometimes, however, there are severe divisions within a church; times when there are two or more factions; times when it seems as if the church is in an uproar and is likely to split, with people going off in different directions to other churches or trying to form a new one.

There can be many reasons for this; there are many potential flashpoints in church life. Some can be mentioned. Sometimes this happens when leaders unwisely insist on some big change, or changes which significant numbers of people are unhappy with. Sometimes it arises when some new teaching or practice comes into the area, either through a new church or some visiting teacher. Sometimes there has been some sin in the church and some members think it has not been dealt with adequately; or alternatively that the guilty person has been dealt with too harshly.

However, whatever the nature of the problem and however serious it seems to be there is grace and wisdom from God to put it right, provided there is willingness for this to happen. There is usually, though, no quick or easy remedy. Four of the seven churches mentioned in Revelation 2 and 3 had very serious problems and the church in Ephesus was also not in a very healthy condition.

However, there were remedies for them all and each had to begin with repentance; a serious turning from all that was wrong back to the Lord himself. The church in the worst condition was that in Laodicea. Nowadays people would be likely to leave such a church and start a new one. However, to the people of that church Jesus gave a glorious promise: 'Behold I stand at the door and knock. If anyone hears my voice and opens the door, I will come in to him and eat with him and he with me' (Revelation 3:20). Even in a church in great trouble believers can still enjoy the presence and fellowship of Christ!

If Jesus was standing at the door of the Laodicean church we can assume that there is a sense in which he stands at the door of every church that is in trouble. As more and more members open their hearts and lives to him, the more the church is renewed and things begin to be put right. But the process is not easy. Members must realise that repentance towards Christ usually also involves confessing to others and asking forgiveness.

Paul's two letters to the church at Corinth are models of seeking to reform and restore church life to what it ought to be. In the first letter he goes through each of the problems and weaknesses of the church, giving advice, showing the members how to put wrongs right and to restore love and fellowship. In the second letter he reveals his heart to them and shows his motives and desires: 'I seek not what is yours but you ... I will most gladly spend and be spent for your souls ... For we are glad when we are weak and you are strong. Your restoration is what we pray for ... Finally, brothers, rejoice. Aim for restoration, comfort one another, agree with one another, live in peace; and the God of love and peace be with you' (2 Corinthians 12:14,15; 13:9,11).

When things go well

Psalm 133 says: 'Behold, how good and pleasant it is when brothers dwell in unity! It is like the precious oil on the head, running down on the beard of Aaron, running down on the collar of his robes! It is like the dew of Hermon, which falls on the mountains of Zion! For there the LORD commanded the blessing, life for evermore.'

When brothers and sisters in the church are united, the fragrance of love and peace flows through the whole church and those who come in cannot but be conscious of it. Such unity is like the dew which causes the flowers and crops to grow and flourish. A united, loving church attracts people to it. It attracts unbelievers who may know very little of joy and love and much of trouble and heartache in their lives.

However, a church on earth is always under attack, the devil sees to that. He wants to spoil its joy, to scatter its members, to prevent it attracting his servants to the Lord's side. Peter speaks like this: 'Be sober-minded; be watchful. Your adversary the devil prowls around like a roaring lion, seeking someone to devour. Resist him, firm in your faith...' (1 Peter 5:8,9). When things go well, watch out for trouble, but trust in the Lord. Do not become proud or complacent. Always press on to serve and glorify Christ.

When things go well a church begins in a small measure to experience a foretaste of what heaven will be like. Heaven is a place of harmony and joy; it is a place where the Triune God is at the centre, where praise wells up from every heart, where God is served with freedom and gladness. It is a place where the sins and sorrows of the past are all forgotten, where the Lamb is on the throne and all hearts are united to love and praise him. Thank God for every such foretaste of glory!

Historically, Baptists took the doctrine of the church very seriously. However, ecclesiology has been the Cinderella of evangelicalism for the past fifty years or more. It is therefore great to see a generation of Baptist pastors once more concerned to argue for and spell out the biblical teaching on the life and order of the local church. This short and accessible book makes an invaluable contribution to the rediscovery of a biblically vibrant local church life. Read it, teach it, study it and put into practice the principles that it expounds.

Robert Strivens, Pastor of Bradford on Avon Baptist Church

It is great to have a book that so positively endorses life in a local church. The authors work from Scripture to paint a picture of what a community of Christians should and can look like. The inner reality of genuine Christian experience is matched with the proper ordering and structuring of that life so that a thriving church is the result. It has long been my conviction that we need to marry, in effect, an 'Acts 2' description of church life with an 'Acts 6' development of good structure. This book takes that idea and works it out much more widely, and with reference to many issues. Anyone interested in seeing their church grow more healthily would benefit from reading this. Warmly commended.

Ray Evans, Lead Minister of Grace Community Church, Kempston

Where can I learn how the church I attend should be structured and run today? Obviously, if we are biblical Christians, we must turn to the Bible. It is great to get some help, however. The Bible itself teaches us that. These essays will do that. They will help pastors and other serious Christians to think through the fundamental issues that have somehow been forgotten or blurred in people's minds down the years. You may not accept every word they write (they do not necessarily want you to) but you will be driven back to the Bible and what it teaches about church (which they do want) and that can only be for your good. I warmly commend this compact and thought-provoking collection of essays.

Gary Brady, Pastor of Childs Hill Baptist Church, London

A common assumption among church leaders today is that the Bible has little to say on organizing and leading our churches. In a respectful and charitable tone, these pastor theologians demonstrate otherwise.

My honest opinion is that this book provides exactly what evangelical Christianity needs, but generally doesn't know it: a biblical vision for robust and healthy churches. Not only that, the authors' pastoral wisdom will encourage and challenge readers on every page. Buy two copies – one for yourself and another for a fellow church leader. I'm confident you'll be glad you did. So will your church.

Jonathan Leeman, Editorial Director, 9Marks

In our time the word church has become somewhat inflated: 'church planting', 'church growth', 'church unity', 'church renewal' are all common expressions that can be found across the board of the evangelical movement and the ecumenical world. The problem is: which church? What is the church? Where is the church? The confusion around the word church is massive. I welcome this rich collection of essays defining, illustrating, and commending the biblical model of a 'pure church', the confessing church, the church made of believers who covenant with one another before God. In Italy there is a growing movement of confessional and confessing churches who will benefit from this book. And I am sure that this will also be the case for many more churches around Europe.

Leonardo De Chirico, Pastor of Breccia di Roma Church, Rome, lecturer in historical theology at IFED and Director of the Reformanda Initiative

The renewal of interest in Baptist ecclesiology in recent years has been the cause of much rejoicing among members of Grace Baptist churches in the UK. Articles have been written. Books have been published. Conferences have been organised. One thing, however, is worth noting. A lot of the available material has had a distinctly American accent.

I realise truth is truth regardless of accent, but it is helpful to hear those truths articulated by those who have not only similar biblical convictions but who share the same cultural context as well.

Written at an accessible level in a warm and engaging manner, these writers – all based in the UK – clearly communicate the gospel order they desire to see recovered by the churches. This work is not just for leaders but for church members as well.

You may not agree with every position taken. But you will be hard-pressed to fault the disposition of the writers. They have sought to write wisely and winsomely for the glory of God and the good of the churches.

Barry King, Pastor of Dunstable Baptist Church and General Secretary of Grace Baptist Partnership

A prayerful spirit breathes through this book, which is characterised by gentleness, humility, energy, joy – and deep conviction. It is written by eleven seasoned pastors who love God's word and know how to teach it clearly, practically and with helpful illustrations. They believe that the more closely local churches order themselves in God's way, the more clearly they will display the gospel. This can only be done by maintaining the intimate connection that exists between conversion, baptism, church membership and the Lord's Supper. If the biblical teaching of this book is read, pondered and put into practice, our congregations will be holy and happy, growing in godliness to the glory of God.

Stuart Olyott, pastor, author and missionary

Here is a fresh, thoughtful and challenging restatement of a classic Baptist understanding of church order for a new generation. Recently there has been a renewal of thinking about ecclesiology among Reformed or Calvinistic Baptists and this book is a fine example. It is accessible and could be used by study groups in churches with much benefit. While not agreeing with everything in it, the book made me think and appreciate more how the manifold wisdom of God is displayed for his glory in local assemblies of Christians. Take and read.

Ken Brownell, Pastor of ELT Baptist Church, Mile End, London

This excellent little book is proof that independency need not mean isolation! Eleven men – all practitioners, not theorists – join up the dots for a compelling picture of church structure that is biblical, practical and inspirational. Full of real life scenarios, and ideal for stimulating discussion, it clearly answers the charge that 'it doesn't matter how we "do church"'. Jesus promised to build his church; the blended voices in this book give straightforward, helpful insights into the Lord's blueprint.

Phil Heaps, one of the elders at Grace Church, Yate

Everything in gospel order

1. The visible church
2. Conversion
3. Baptism
4. Membership
5. The Lord's Supper
6. Discipleship
7. Discipline
8. Independency
9. Leadership
10. Gospel unity

Contents

The #TitusOneFive Statement

Reaffirming the biblical connection between conversion, baptism, church membership and the Lord's Supper

Local churches should be like cities set on hills (Matt. 5:14): gospel communities made up of those saved by the grace of God, recreated by him, and displaying to the watching world the breaking in of God's kingdom of love, righteousness and joy. We want to equip churches to have a biblical vision of this reality, so that the light of Christ might not only be proclaimed, but seen ever more brightly in our generation.

We believe that the biblical elements of a 'gospel order' (conversion, baptism, church membership and the Lord's Supper), ministered lovingly and correctly, together reveal these spiritual realities, and hence become the framework in which a gospel community can thrive.

Doctrinally, we take an evangelical stance as set out in the historic Reformed Baptist confessions, and in addition we hold to the following beliefs and practices relating to gospel order:

1. We believe that the universal church is the body of which Christ is the head, to which all who are saved belong, and that it is made visible in local churches – organised gatherings of Christians – who are:

    i. united by a statement of faith which expresses the doctrines believed by the church, which are often highlighted, and agreed by every believer who comes into church membership;

    ii. fed and shaped by the ministry of the word as the focus of their life together in Christ as a gathered church, aided by the gospel signs of baptism and communion.

2. We believe that a Christian is someone who has been genuinely converted by God. Conversion is radical, and occurs when God gives life to spiritually dead people. It is evidenced in the gifts of personal faith in Jesus Christ and repentance from sin.

3. We believe that baptism is:

    i. a local church's act of affirming and portraying a converted person's union with Christ by immersing him or her in water;

    ii. a converted person's act of publicly committing him or herself to Christ and his people, thereby uniting them to the church and marking them off from the world;

    iii. the act which commences a converted person's membership of a local church.

4. We believe that anyone wishing to join a local church should be given opportunity to understand the responsibilities and joys of church membership, and thus agree to the church's statement of faith and the values that govern their life together (perhaps evidenced by the signing of a church covenant). Admission to membership can then occur, after:

    i. the church has affirmed the candidate's profession of faith, evidenced by an explanation of their conversion and the gospel;

    ii. the candidate has been baptised as a believer.

5. We believe that the Lord's Supper is:

    i. a local church's act of communing with Christ and each other, and of commemorating Christ's death by partaking of bread and wine;

    ii. a converted, baptised person's act of receiving Christ's benefits and renewing his or her commitment to Christ and his people;

    iii. Christ's ongoing means of binding the members of a local church together as one body and marking it off from the world;

    iv. for baptised members of local churches, whether members of the church where the Supper is being celebrated, or visitors in good standing at another gospel church.

6. We believe that each local church should be characterised by a shared life of discipleship. As all the members are equipped, they should be encouraged to use their gifts to serve others in various works of ministry and prayer. Together, each local church is to grow in holiness as Christ's bride and in witness as his ambassadors to the watching world. Local church life is to be a growing display of heaven on earth.

7. We believe that church discipline is a provision of Christ for the protection of the honour of his name in a local church. This removal from church membership, and withholding of the Lord's Supper, may become necessary against any church member whose life or doctrine renders their profession of faith in Christ incredible. It is used after much pastoral care, and in order that the offender might be brought back to repentance and faith, and afterwards gladly readmitted to church membership.

8. We believe that each local church has final authority to admit and dismiss members, appoint and remove leaders, and establish the doctrinal and moral standards of the church. These processes should be implemented at regular church members' meetings.
9. We believe that each local church should be led, taught, and prayed over by a plurality of godly and suitably gifted elders, as defined in the Pastoral Epistles, and served by similarly godly deacons, who, for the sake of unity, and for the upholding of the ministry of the word, are to care for particular needs arising in the life of the church.
10. We believe that meaningful fellowship between local churches exists where there is evident faithfulness to the gospel, and that for the sake of displaying unity churches should look to foster good relationships with all other gospel-preaching churches within their locality.

We present these principles in a spirit of submission to the word of God, in acknowledgement of our need of ongoing reform by the Spirit, and in hope of the promotion of warm gospel unity among many.

Soli Deo Gloria.

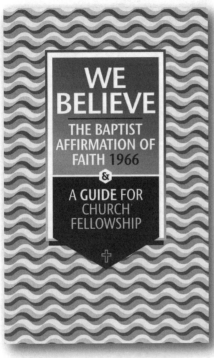

WE BELIEVE
THE BAPTIST AFFIRMATION OF FAITH 1966
A GUIDE FOR CHURCH FELLOWSHIP
ISBN 978-1-912154-07-4
Paperback, 112 pages, £4.99

Christian Books
Ashton Square St Mary's Gate,
Dunstable, Beds. LU6 3SW.
Telephone 01582 601945
www.christianbooks.uk.com
email: books@christianbooks.uk.com

This publication is made up of two historic documents which were approved by the Strict Baptist Assembly: *The 1966 Baptist Affirmation of Faith* and *The Assembly Guide for Church Fellowship*.

The Grace Baptist Assembly, which succeeded the earlier Assembly, commends these documents to the churches.

It is hoped they will contribute to the grounding of the churches in the faith and stimulate a continuing reformation of life.

Grace
Publications